Not Yet!

Tales From a 90-Year-Old Broadway Diva You Should Have Known

Sally-Jane Heit

Beansprout Productions

Not Yet!

Cover Design by Lynnette Najimy
Editing by Tamara Jones and Lynnette Najimy

Publisher: Beansprout Productions, LLC

ISBN: 979-8-9910179-0-9

Also Available as e-book and audiobook

Advance Praise

In this insightful, brave, breathtakingly hilarious book, actor Sally-Jane Heit looks back at age 90 on an eventful, tumultuous life driven, and possibly ruined, by her insatiable need for attention.

Stardom eludes her at every turn. One-woman shows flop. Big Broadway chances evaporate. Along the way, the brassy performer learns to relish her days in summer stock and being the Queen of the dinner-theater circuit. Actors will surely relate, but Heit's personal stories will astonish and delight any reader. From her early experiences with romance and sex to her theatrical misadventures, the laugh-out-loud moments abound.

A natural storyteller and truth-addict, Heit leaves it all on the page. She doesn't just grow on you; she gets inside you. Before you know it, you've fallen for her. Don't miss this first-person account of a wild and wonderful life. You've never read anything like it.

Martha Sherrill, Author of *My Last Movie Star* and *Dog Man, An Uncommon Life on a Faraway Mountain*

Writer, actor, singer and outsize personality, Sally-Jane has lived life to the full. Family, friends and lovers have found it hard to keep pace with her exuberance.

As her delightful and entertaining memoir shows she has been happiest when performing. Her one-woman show, a demonstration of feminine angst bolstered by sharp observations on the human predicament, kept audiences entertained from New York to London.

Her honesty, though sometimes painful, shines through. Sally-Jane has inspired great love. Long may she continue to do so.

Barry Turner, British Author & Historian

Contents

Dedication

This book is dedicated, with unconditional love, to three beautiful, creative, amazing women of the world who happened to be my daughters, Dianne, Lori, and Pamela

Epigraph

Maturity begins with the capacity to sense and, in good time and without defensiveness, admit to our own craziness. If we are not regularly deeply embarrassed by who we are, the journey to self-knowledge hasn't begun.

From *The Course of Love*
by Alain de Botton

Prologue

L aying in a hospital bed listening to the whirring, beeping, and flashing of the monitors that are meant to keep me alive, I had one thought...

I can't die yet.
I haven't been discovered.

It was 2022, and I was an 89-year-old woman with serious health conditions. It would surprise no one if I kicked the bucket before completing my bucket list.

Top on that list, from the nine months in my mother's womb right up to this fateful day, what I wanted was to be hailed by the world as a Star.

There wasn't an era in my life that wasn't covered by a desperate wannabe dream. From Shirley Temple to Judy Garland to Betty Grable to Carol Channing. Would you believe Whoopi Goldberg? I challenged each of these ladies to an imaginary talent contest, which I have always won.

As it is wont to do, reality got in the way. I was just another 1950s girl in Bert Lahr's Cowardly Lion costume. I lacked the courage of my silent convictions. I wasn't the first, and I won't be the last female who tried to have it all... balancing marriage, children, and work.

My marriage to a workaholic with a wandering eye was helpful until it wasn't. Over the years, my three daughters were the ballast that righted my oftentimes sinking ship.

No matter how conflicted I was, I never stopped working or looking for someone to take me somewhere over that rainbow.

When I felt my body was no longer capable of doing my best, at age 84, I performed my last one-woman show.

Thank you, Mr. Dylan Thomas. I did not go gently into that dark night. My need to put my two cents into any discussion, debate, or dialogue on any subject, even when nobody asked me, found its creative home in my *Blah, Blah, Blog*. A good friend kept pushing me to write a memoir.

Who the hell would publish, no less read, a book about Sally-Jane What's-Her-Name? In the publishing world, the days of discovering hidden, unknown talents were over. Celebrity and books with a hook became the way of the publishing world. I wasn't a bastard child of some foreign prince who turned up on Jerry Springer in search of my long-lost father.

I confess. Writing a memoir was not a new idea for me. Of course, this big-mouthed, know-it-all wanted to tell it like it was. At 89, there were so many challenges. Would I be able to tell my version of the truth without blame or shame? Did I have the physical stamina? The latter question was easier to answer than the former. The light of creativity would go out with my last breath... from my mouth to God's ears.

I did have enough breath to write my story, share a few mixed opinions and judgments, and keep my arthritic fingers and absurd mental meanderings moving around a keyboard.

Could I write my story and finally be discovered as the Grandma Moses of the printed word? Perform readings and book signings? Be interviewed on NPR's *Fresh Air*? Be on the cover of *People* or *Time*?

Oh, God, doesn't it sound wonderful?

It sure sounds like I was trying to convince myself, doesn't it?

I was being released from the hospital. As the nurse removed the bells and whistles of my hook-up, I looked up at the sign on the door of my hospital room:

Fall Precautions
Fluid Restriction
Heart Failure

WHAT?????

I spent most of my life dining at the same table with Mel Brooks and his *2,000 Year Old Man*, waiting, waiting, waiting for the Angel from Death. I couldn't believe what I was reading.

While I was still alive and breathing, like a horror movie, the medical establishment was counting me out! I wasn't even dead yet, and they were burying me.

I get it. My shelf life is unknown to me. But the world wants to count me out before I am counted out.

Like the Brooks/Reiner *2,000 Year Old Man*, my only protection against the Angel from Death is a necklace of fresh garlic I wear every night when I go to bed. One sniff and the angel takes off like a bat out of hell.

The sign on the door was another unfortunate medical mashup. Obviously, it belonged to the guy next door.

Beyond all reason, a state I am most familiar with, I needed to stay alive.

Why? Because any minute, I am going to be discovered.

Sally-Jane! Get your ass out of this bed now!

I'm going to print a new sign for all my doors...

NOT YET!

That is not a bad title for a memoir.

Whoa! Am I actually going to do this? Talk about climbing a sand mountain.

I was born the seventh cliché in a family of eight cliché's, living with our chief cliché's, Mother and Father. We were raised on such gems as, "Sally-Jane, a rolling stone is hard on the kidneys."

There are no new stories. We are each living variations of the same ol', same ol'. This is definitely true about my story. It's so damn repetitive and clichéd. Sex, stardom, marriage, sex, parenting, sex, stardom, sex, travel, sex, divorce, and most importantly, the childhood trauma that gave me a passport to be a very sophisticated neurotic. You do know the difference between a neurotic and a psychotic, don't you? A neurotic is someone who builds castles in the air. A psychotic is someone who moves in.

Sorry. I just had to. It's one of my favorites, and it is so apropos.

Wait a minute. Does this mean what I think it means?
I have always believed that God takes care of fools.
I'm still here. So it must be true.

A memoir can only be written by me, right?
I have to be alive to write it, right?

I'm not going to worry about truth or stamina. However, if my time is called before... well, you know...

Do me a favor, please.

Do what I am doing. Make it up and finish the damn thing while I add another sign to my door:

WELCOME

...to my story.

A Bowl of Cherries Ends in the Pits

T he night before my wedding, my mother went batshit.
"Sally-Jane, if you marry Richard, your life will be over."

We were seated at the dining room table, going over the seating chart.

"Aunt Miriam will never sit next to Aunt Lily," my mother complained.
"Maybe someone can tell her to use some mouthwash."
"That isn't why."
"Well, that's why I wouldn't sit next to her.
"Sally-Jane, it's not too late."
"What's not?"
"Don't marry Richard."
"That's not funny, mother."
"I mean it."
"What are you talking about? You love Richard."
"Ludvig! I love Ludvig. He played piano beautifully."
"What are you talking about? You loved his Princeton... his Yale Law School."
"I didn't. I don't. If you marry Richard, your life will be over."

She picked herself up off the chair and calmly walked out of the room, up the stairs to her bedroom, undressed, found the concave spot in the mattress that was hers next to her (unaware in every possible way) husband and my father, and promptly went to sleep.

She left me still seated at the table, holding what was now a useless seating chart. Bubbles and gurgles of fear and panic made their way through the various canals of my gut to my lungs as I gasped for breath and tried not to throw up. After detonating her bomb on my person, my mother stepped away from my remains and went to bed. The night before my wedding, my own mother murdered me. I had always suspected she didn't love me. But this... this... did she ever love me?

I was born in 1933, amidst the Great Depression. I grew up in a house that was always a war zone. Four boys, four girls, each of us in a life-and-death battle for parental attention.

The roost I was born into was ruled by a 5-foot tall, strong, stubborn supermom who, for her own purposes, before you asked the question, knew the answer. The early loss of her mother left her with a terror of not knowing. Knowing everything was life. Not knowing was death.

I had known this woman for over 19 years. In that time, she had perpetrated some dastardly deeds. This prayer, curse, whatever it was she threw at me the night before my wedding was the worst.

To be truthful, which most of the time was against my better judgment, my mind unconsciously agreed with her pronouncement. I didn't want to get married. It was the only plan of escape I could think of to get away from my family and mostly my mother.

What to do? Oh, God, I was so confused.

Finally, at 3 a.m. I telephoned Richard and announced, "I'm not getting married today."

When Sondheim later wrote *I'm Not Getting Married Today* for the musical, *Company*, it always had special meaning for me.

"Richard, I am so sorry. I can't possibly get married today. Please tell your parents. They can call your family. You can call your friends. I'll do the same for my side."
"Sally-Jane! Are you serious?"
"Never been more in my life."
"I'm coming right over."

I didn't have time to tell him he couldn't see the bride before the wedding. It didn't matter since there wasn't going to be any wedding.

He didn't have to ring the bell. I was sitting on the steps in front of my house, crying. What a mess.

He was kind and considerate in the extreme. Richard had never been like this before. In so many ways, he was just like my mother. He never asked a question he didn't already have the answer for. But tonight, he was different. He asked, "What happened?"

He wiped away my tears. He put his arm around my shoulder, and this time it wasn't for the surreptitious quick feel of my boobs.

I explained that we were working on the seating arrangements. Placing Aunt Lily anywhere was always a problem. He sat next to her at our engagement dinner, so he understood.

Between sobs, I cried, "She told me if I married you, my life would be over."

I cried harder and buried myself in his Ivy League blazer. He pulled me closer to him, and like Irene Dunne in *I Remember Mama*, he comforted me. It felt so strange.

"Oh, Sally-Jane. Can't you see what's happening?"

"Of course. She hates me. She's always hated me, even when I was a good girl, even when I got the part, even when I won the Belle of the Borough contest. She always loved anyone better than me... especially Arlene and Elliot."

"No, honey, she doesn't hate you. Her children are leaving home. Raymond, Allyn, Marilyn, Elliot... who comes after Elliot?"

"Lucille..."

"Lucille, David, and now you. Arlene is the only one left. She is very sad. When one of your brothers or sisters married, there were always leftovers. When you get married tomorrow, she will have only one child left. She wants you to marry me. She doesn't want to be alone without her children."

Oh, my God, he was so smart. How could he be so smart and still live?

He was so damn soothing. And he was holding me. And he was petting me. Not sexually petting me – like petting a good dog petting me. He painted a lovely and sad picture. He promised he would always take care of me. He would protect me from my mother. He would let me do whatever I wanted to do. He always wanted to know what I was doing. My mother always wanted to know what I was doing. But this was different. Richard only wanted to know because he loved me. My mother didn't love me. She made that eminently clear this evening.

He left me on the stoop with a dry kiss. Thank goodness. I really hated the other kind.

A few hours later, having packed my bridal gown, a store-bought above-ankle white lace dress with a white silk cumberbund, a crown and veil, Capezio white satin shoes with a cross band of fake pearls, my something old - a handkerchief worn by my best friend at her wedding, something new - a string of cultured pearls that my mother had presented to me a few days before her curse, something blue - a store-bought blue garter. I also packed my Loehmann's (a high-end discount fashion store) very smart going-away suit and white gloves and going-away bag packed with trousseau items of silk and lace underwear, nightgown and peignoir, satin slippers with feather pom-poms. Richard and I were going off for a few days before we traveled to Montreal, where we were to board a slow boat to Le Havre, where our honeymoon would officially begin.

My mother and father and younger sister Arlene, my maid of honor, drove into New York City to the Gotham Hotel on 5th Avenue and 55th Street. It was a smaller but beautiful old hotel a few blocks from the bigger and fancier Plaza and Pierre.

In fearful excitement, I dressed as the photographer took the prescribed photos of the bride dressing with Mother, soon-to-be mother-in-law, sisters, and friends in attendance. As the minutes ticked by, the excitement built. The confusion and fog of the trauma and anxiety of the previous hours disappeared as the heat from the spotlight focused all its brilliance on me. As I placed the crown encircled by the veil upon my head, I knew not only that I was the star of my own show, but I was Queen for this day.

At the rear of the ballroom, I waited with my father, who played a magnificent Father of the Bride, a role he was born for and which he played once before with my sister Marilyn. (Lucille had married out of the religion, robbing him of a chance to do what he does so well: play somebody else.)

The ballroom had been arranged theatre-style with a beautiful floral chuppah, a canopy of colorful summer greenery, and flowers placed at the end of a red-carpeted aisle. The rabbi stood under it, waiting for the procession to begin. Richard's best man, followed by my sister Arlene, followed by Richard being held up on one side by his mother and on the other side by his father. A perfect picture of a dead man walking.

Then, the moment of moments, the quartet struck up the beginning chords of *Mendelssohn's Bridal March*.
The whole damned audience stood up.
I hadn't done anything, and yet they stood up.
My first standing ovation.

At that moment, mysterious hands passed the bridal bouquet to mine. It was gorgeous: white stephanotis surrounded by trailing white mini orchids set on a white satin bible (to match my shoes) imprinted with my name. I put my arm through my father's arm. I do not think we even looked at each other. He had his part and knew what to do, and I had mine. Walking down the aisle like a queen, I dispensed smiles and benevolences as I passed – first one side of the aisle, then the other side. There wasn't a bride alive who milked each moment at her wedding performance better'n me... ever.

When Richard and I exchanged our vows, you may not have heard him, but there was no way I wasn't heard. In a voice trained by the best and speaking trippingly on the tongue, I promised to love, honor, and obey until death do us part.

Over the next twenty-seven years, intentionally or not, one of us or the other or sometimes together betrayed every one of those promises except death. Death has its own timing.

The rabbi asked me to repeat after him, and as I did, the cord that should have been cut from mother to daughter at birth detached. When Richard raised his foot and stomped down hard, shattering the glass beneath it, a Jewish wedding tradition symbolically representing the destruction of the Temple in Jerusalem, so too, I thought the separation from daughter to parent was complete.

After changing into my going-away ensemble with a small veiled hat and white gloves, color coordinated and matching handbag and shoes, waving and throwing kisses, I made my way through the revolving door of the hotel where friends attached the *Just Married* sign and tin cans to our waiting convertible.

I did it. I escaped.

Oh, yes, how could I forget? I kept my part of the deal. Richard finally had his way with me. As my friend Harriet Ferment always said,

"Every virgin forest needs a man to cut her down."

2

The Great Escape

It's hard to say which of us entered marriage more clueless. What was truly ridiculous was each of us, consciously or unconsciously, thought we were successfully manipulating the other.

Richard was not aware that he had been chosen to rescue me, so I thought. What he didn't know wouldn't hurt him, and if he ever found out, I was a practiced liar. Poetically speaking, I thought I was the sculptor, and he was my clay. What can I tell you? I was a really dumb eighteen-year-old.

It will come as no surprise to anyone that an eighteen-year-old who thinks she has control of anything is hilarious. Much later, I laughed at myself for trying to control what could not be controlled. It took me years to realize that the decades of my brilliant manipulations were being canceled out by Richard's much more brilliant manipulations.

He had the major advantage of the particular era we were living in. He was a he. When I met Richard in 1951, feminism was a nascent dream. James Brown was right—it's *A Man's World*!

Richard made it clear to me that his classical education at Princeton made him a superior being. His academic discipline intimidated me. The study of history, politics, and philosophy was alien to my quest for stardom. And he was curious. Oh, God, was he curious... about everything. He never stopped asking questions. Richard had no middle name, but if he had one, it would have been *Questions*: *Richard Questions!* He didn't have conversations. He asked questions. Sometimes, it felt like a simple quest for information. Sometimes, it was like living with Torquemada during the Spanish Inquisition. It took me many years before I realized that asking questions can be used as manipulation.

For me, education was unimportant. Going to school was a waiting game until discovery. Betty Grable didn't have a degree in anything except how to look gorgeous in a one-piece white bathing suit, back turned, looking over her shoulder. Before Richard, I felt no need to explore anything beyond the world of show business.

Every day of the two months before Richard left for the Army, we went out in his father's van, delivering tires and other products from his father's successful tire business. He drove. I sat on the floor of the van. The seat had been removed to increase the space for deliveries.

We talked—I mean, he talked. Sometimes, I responded to a question, but usually, his question led to another question. I learned to be quick. He was quicker.

Sitting on the floor of the van made it so picture-perfect. As he expounded about this subject or that, I looked *up* at him. Precisely! I was a disciple in the making. I was dazzled by the breadth of his knowledge. From his questions, I understood how smart he was and how smart I wasn't. As we traveled and delivered merchandise, I lost control of controlling Richard.

It wasn't a complete loss. The side of the brain that searches for meaning and understanding was stimulated. Suddenly, like *Alice in Wonderland*, I became curiouser and curiouser. And it wasn't about show business. I had always loved books. Growing up, they were my best friends. Books of escape, fairy tales, *Nancy Drew*, occasional biographies of stars of the theatre and musical worlds. Most important were the movie magazines. They contained the discovery stories that fueled my dreams.

As Richard's influence over me grew, my reading list changed. I never gave up the movie and gossip magazines but I added classical literature and histories, all of which I discovered I really enjoyed. Reading became challenging and stimulating. As he kept reminding me, I was fortunate to have met him. For him, Hunter College was not to be mentioned in the same breath as Princeton.

It didn't take long before I found that I was eternally grateful that Richard had rescued *me* from a fate worse than a *free* education.

Fortunately for me, Richard committed himself to playing Henry Higgins to my Liza Doolittle. Unfortunately for me, he was born a male with one of those "things" between his legs. As a child, I was sexually abused, so that "thing" frightened the bejesus out of me. Throughout all the many years of my pathological denial of my abuse, I made it my business not to know how the lower part of my body worked. Below my waist was a wasteland. I didn't have any idea what any parts of my anatomy were for and furthermore, I didn't want to know. My greatest acting triumphs were me playing the sexy vamp. Man, I could swing and sway my hips, pout, and pucker my lips. The only thing I couldn't do was flip my hair because it was too damn curly.

For me and other ladies of the 1950s, sex was our only bargaining chip in a world market that was stacked against us. My virginity was highly praised and priced.

In the 1950s, in so-called Western civilized countries, being a virgin was still important. Make no mistake, I was no princess or heiress. However, my most prized value on the open marriage market was my virginity. It was my ticket out and away from my family. Fort Knox was not as secure as my chastity belt.

I had selected Richard as my rescuer. I was a 1950 *girl* with a giant bravura ego, no self-esteem, and a big dream. At 18, my only ace was my virginity. There was no way I was going to give that away without the assurance that this guy was serious and would actually save me. A not-so-minor factor was my mother.

"Sally-Jane! If you so much as unbutton a button or lower your bloomers I will know. God help you! I will take you on the subway to the island in the middle of the East River where the indigent and the insane live, leave you, and take the subway home without you."

Literally, as push came to shove, as Richard tried to go "all the way," panting and promising he'd still respect me, I cried.

"STOP! I can't. I want to. I really want to. This is as difficult for me as it is for you (big joke). But I made a promise to my mother. I swore I would only give myself to the man I love and respect and who loved and respected me in sickness and in health, for richer or for poorer, 'til death do us part."

It was Academy Award-worthy.

In 1954, our two separate paths would converge in bed, where I promised him my virginity and a good time only after we were married.

And that, my friends, is how, on June 20, 1954, I fooled myself and Richard and entered the bondage of marriage.

3

The Honeylessmoon

After the wedding, we had ten days before our boat left for France. We spent those days returning wedding gifts and counting and recounting our money. For $500, if we were very careful and literally counted every penny, we could do our version of a three-month European tour. What that really meant was if we starved, bought most of our food from markets, found a cheap car rental, slept in the car, in youth hostels, or strange rooms in strangers' houses, we could depart.

Our passage to France via small ship and our return flight was booked and paid for through student charter organizations. All other monies were for food and shelter and tchotchkes. Can't come home without a little something for everyone.

It was an interesting time to visit Europe – the understatement of the Century: ten years after D-Day and the end of World War II. The devastation, physically and psychologically, of war was everywhere. Here is another understatement. In preparing for this journey, that fact never occurred to Richard or me. In my headball, I was following Hemingway and Fitzgerald, not Patton and Eisenhower. Before we left, reality reared its ugly head. We asked Richard's parents for more money. They agreed – on one condition.

"Do not go to Germany. Do not buy anything made in Germany."

I don't remember either family ever talking about the Holocaust. It was a subject for the history books. Obviously, in our families if you didn't talk about it, it didn't happen. We were so very young and so very dumb.

With our fingers crossed behind our backs, we promised we wouldn't go to Germany.

Our small boat took nine days to go from Montreal to the French port of Le Havre. The ship had only two classes: first class (hah!) and steerage (HAH! HAH!) Steerage had only upper and lower bunks, thereby limiting our conjugal visits. I was thrilled.

I was completely involved with creating my own tour of the Continent. In my mind, I was joining E.M. Forster, Edith Wharton, F. Scott Fitzgerald, Gertrude Stein, Hemingway, and others who "did the continent" before me. Each city and country we traveled to would add depth and breadth to my artistry. I may have lost my virginity, but I was on my way to becoming an artist of consequence.

After arriving in Le Havre, the first order of business was to find a cheap car rental. Inflation was rampant. France was ridiculously expensive. We took the train to Belgium and then on to Holland, both also out of reach for our budget. The man in Holland took pity on us and suggested that if we were willing to go to Germany, he knew of someone who was just starting a car rental business, and because he was a German in Germany, he didn't have many customers. What about our promise? Richard decided his father would understand. He was a businessman. Besides, our fingers were crossed behind our backs.

Our first experience in Germany was mind-boggling. No matter where we went or who we were dealing with, it appeared there were no Germans in Germany during World War II. They were all on the Russian front. No one, and I mean *no one*, wanted to admit they were in Germany during the Nazi regime. They did not know what happened until it was all over. Amazing.

The car rental dealer spoke English. I was about to ask where he learned English. Richard stopped me. He thought that if Germans didn't want to admit that they were in Germany during World War II, they probably didn't want to be questioned.

Our Volkswagen license plate had a Big D, which indicated it was from Deutschland, aka Germany. We were turned away from many hostels and hotels before we understood that it wasn't us, but the country where the car was from that was being rejected. Like Richard's parents, many Europeans wanted nothing to do with Germans.

I did not like the taste of wine. Richard added this to the growing list of my negative character traits:

Aversion to sex. (he had a point)
Free college. (Princeton was better)
Can't count. (blame free college education)
Hates wine. (bottle of vin ordinaire 10 cents; Coca-Cola $1)

We were traveling from Vichy en route to the French Riviera and Monte Carlo. I was so excited. I had my bathing "costume," my sandals, my dark glasses, and a couple of extra francs for un petit chemin de fer at the casino. But first a stop at the market in Vichy for what was our standard breakfast and lunch, a baguette and accompanying cheese.

Richard pulled up outside the market. As keeper of the purse, he counted out some francs and sent me forth. After the baguette was bought, I headed toward the cheese section of the market. Atop the sign of what looked like Swiss cheese to me was another sign that read 1 kilo, 10 c. I translated that to mean 1 kilo for ten centimes. Yes! We definitely could afford ten centimes. I hadn't the foggiest idea what a kilo was... if there was more after breakfast and lunch, we could use it for snacks. Only later I learned that one kilo was the equivalent of two and a half pounds of cheese.

I pointed to the "Swiss cheese," and the cheesemonger took his knife and cut off a huge block – enough for an army. This was a very good deal. However, we didn't have anything to cut the cheese into portions, so in pantomime, I requested that the cheesemonger chop up the huge piece of cheese into chunks small enough to fit into a pull of bread. I had excelled in my pantomime class. He understood.

Shaking his head and smiling to himself, thinking, "Crazy American," he proceeded to cut the huge chunk of cheese into small pieces. He wrapped my huge pile of cut-up cheese into paper. I then took out my ten-centimes and gave them to him.

He looked questioningly at the money and said, "Non!"

I pointed to the sign. He shook his head. He took out his black pencil, erased the c, and added a zero to the ten and the letter F. It wasn't ten centimes. It was 100 francs.

Richard would kill me. I looked around. People being people always had a scent for a scene. They were gathering. I kept repeating the one word I was sure would be understood.

"Non! Non! Non!"

The cheesemonger was getting more and more frustrated. I began to back away. Slowly, at first, afraid of being attacked. With my baguette under my arm, I made a dash towards the exit and Richard in our waiting car.

The cheesemonger, carrying 2 ½ pounds of cut-up Swiss cheese, ran after me screaming, "Crazy American! Crazy American!"

I got to the car. Opened the door, yelling, "Richard, don't ask. We have to get out of here now!"

As the cheesemonger waved his cheese and screamed, he was accompanied by fellow marketers always primed for a good Market Day story. Richard hit the gas pedal, and we were off in a cloud of carbon dioxide. After explaining what happened, Richard did have the good grace to laugh but never let me go into a market alone again.

Before Vichy, there was Paris. Forget the Eiffel Tower or the Place de Concord, the Louvre. If we were to eat, we needed to find a cheap hotel room. Richard, a former Eagle Scout, could read a compass or a map. I'm a Brooklyn girl who took the subway or a bus — books, not maps.

His hands had to be free to read the map. In Eagle Scout style, he tied all our luggage onto my body, walking ahead with his trusty magnifying glass pressed against the Paris street map while I slowly trailed behind, dragging my luggage-laden body. For hours, we walked in and out, up and down the side streets of the Left Bank.

Because there were so few hotels, rooms were more expensive, and not too many people spoke English. My years of high school and college French were supposed to do the trick. There were some difficulties. My French was a Sid Caesar *Show of Shows* nonsense accented French. I always threw in an occasional real French word to further confuse my listener. I could mimic the French mouth and gestures. It sounded and looked like I was speaking French. I threw in real words like mon Dieu, sacre bleu, and bien sur, which, for the French person listening, made my nonsense even more nonsensical. Much worse and almost impossible was whenever numbers were introduced into the negotiation. Eventually, we found the cheapest room on the Left Bank, a fifth-floor walkup.

I wish I could tell you that once the luggage was unstrapped from my body, I asked for a divorce. Are you kidding? Even as this beast of burden walked the streets of the Left Bank and climbed the five stories, I was so grateful to be married to Richard. He knew how to do everything. I was one lucky, silly, not-very-bright new wife. How had I managed my life before I met him?

The bigger question is how I allowed this to happen. When I walked down the aisle, I thought I had engineered the great escape. I was free. In reflection, I think what I really meant was that I was free to gerrymander my old umbilical cord and reconnect it to Richard.

The blanket acceptance of whatever Richard proposed covered an unconscious fear, ugly, ugly fear, that began probably in 1933. It's called "birth canal trauma." Don't knock what you don't know. That fear was exacerbated in 1936 when, along with my brother David, we were abandoned and again in 1954 as I stepped off the gangplank in France.

As a child, I was able to manipulate, lie, and cheat my way through my parents' attempts to control my life. I was surrounded by familiar territory and people. After the wedding, at 19, I found myself across the ocean in strange places with strange people with whom I had a very limited ability to communicate. I was traveling with a strange man I thought I knew but whom I knew I did not know. Stockholm Syndrome. The honeymoon, in so many ways, was a shock to an over-sensitive nervous system. Daily, I was confronted with people I didn't understand, who didn't understand me, and whose lives had been decimated by war. I was of an age and part of a protected and privileged American generation where English and European degradation had not been part of my life experience. I went to the movies regularly but always skipped the newsreels and war movies.

Musicals, horror movies, and fantasies only, please. I had three brothers in the service. My service to them was recording patriotic World War II songs to be sent to them "over there." In my archives, somewhere, is a recording of me singing *Let's Remember Pearl Harbor* and *Praise The Lord and Pass The Ammunition*. I knew about rationing. I gathered metal and newspapers for "the war effort." I didn't connect the dots. I was soooo ignorant. It wasn't talked about in elementary school, and it wasn't talked about at home. In junior high school, I remember visiting a friend who had a flag with a gold star hanging from her window. I never asked what that meant.

As a newlywed nineteen-year-old, I was embarrassed and ashamed about how much of nothing I knew. And I was beyond grateful that Richard was there to hold my hand and navigate the dangerous tides and currents of this unknown world. It was with gratitude and, I thought, love that I gave over more and more of myself to his control. He made me feel safe... safer.

Between the courtship and the marriage, my pseudo-independent life unconsciously morphed into that dreadful relationship disease, codependency.

It is ludicrous and embarrassing. It was 1954. I was in France. Five years before, in 1949, Simone de Beauvoir wrote and published *The Second Sex*, a brilliant and logical plea to accept the equality of men and women.

Now at 19, I had escaped my home and my family only to move into my new home with my new mother-father-guardian-protector.

Phew!
Can you believe it?
I almost made it into my own life.

4

After the Honeylessmoon

After the Honeymoon, I had a job waiting for me as an English/Social Studies teacher in a suburban middle school outside of New Haven. Oh, those poor students. During my time there, they couldn't write a grammatically correct sentence, but they could tell you what shows were coming through New Haven on their way to Broadway. When Richard began his second year at Yale Law School, Yale University undergraduate school was still all male. The Yale Dramat, the undergraduate Drama Club, produced some wonderful theatre. For the two years I taught in New Haven, I became the go-to comedy actress for the Yale Dramat. It satisfied my itch.

We lived in a field of Quonset Huts adjacent to the Yale Bowl. These Quonset huts were housing built after World War II for married veterans attending the many graduate schools at Yale. My first home had a round roof made of tin. In a peculiar way, it seemed to complement my version of playing an average, normal, everyday housewife. Me, normal? This "normal" housewife couldn't boil water. I mean, literally, I put a pot of water on the stove to boil, then I put my hand in the pot to check if bubbling water was the same as boiling water.

In a further attempt to prove I could out-Donna Donna Reed, I wanted to cook something exotic for my new husband—potato salad. If you can't boil water, potato salad is exotic.

The recipe came from a cookbook gifted to me by my mother. That alone should have made me suspicious. I followed the instructions to the letter. I was too terrified to deviate.

I took six potatoes, peeled them, and cut them up. I took two stalks of celery. I cut them up. I didn't know what spring onions were, so I left them out. I mixed together mayonnaise, salt, and pepper with the potatoes and celery, and put it in the salad bowl. I waited for Richard to return from class. I actually wore a costume: Aunt Lily's bridal shower gift of an apron. I tried to return it, but the store wouldn't take it back. I served him the salad.

He took one bite, looked up into my hopeful eyes, and asked, "Are potatoes supposed to be hard?"

I was shattered. I grabbed the bowl and ran sobbing to my next door neighbor. I pushed the bowl under her nose and, between sobs, gaspingly explained what had just happened. She was all sweetness and comfort. Then she took a bite. She broke up into hysterical laughter, almost choking on a potato. I was angry and confused. How could she be so callous?

I cried, "What's so funny?"
"You didn't cook the potatoes!"
"It didn't say to cook the potatoes."
"It didn't say to cook the potatoes because who doesn't know you have to cook the potatoes?"

Well, my friends, that is precisely the point, isn't it? I didn't know potatoes in potato salad were supposed to be cooked because I didn't care enough about cooking potatoes, boiling water, being a housewife. Everything I lived for was in service of being discovered and stardom. Sue me.

Like many law school graduates before him, Richard chose the government agency he would work for in Washington, D.C. As we left the ivy-covered walls of a make-believe married life behind, I felt a shiver of premonition. I had always thought Richard and I were in agreement about our plans for the future. He would work wherever for the first few years. However, eventually, we were going to return to New York City. He would begin his climb to Partnership with a good

New York law firm. I would finally be discovered. If it's not written somewhere, the agreement never existed. I didn't go to law school and even I knew that.

Considering we were two volatile and aggressive personalities, the first five years of our marriage were surprisingly sanguine. Each of us could pursue our pursuits with support and without conflict. How was that even possible?

There were no children.

5

My Dossier

My first memories begin at the age of three. I was the seventh of eight children, one more competitive than the other. My position in the family was solid. I was the monkey grinder's monkey. I could and did perform at the drop of a hat. Every time we had company, I would crawl out from my hiding place under the piano, climb atop the piano bench, and sing, accompanying myself with adorable Shirley Temple-like gestures, first the right hand, then the left hand.

This is pinky
This is pinky
How are you?
How are you?
Very well, I thank you
Very well, I thank you
Run away
Run away

I continued that song through ring man, middle man, pointer, and thumb man.

Aunt Lily whispered to my mother, "Anna! She is the next Shirley Temple."

It was a magical time. There were no hugs or kisses in my family, but being noticed and praised over my sisters and brothers felt like a hundred hugs and kisses.

My mother was very Victorian. Anna did not spare the rod. Going against her will brought a hard cheek pinch or a comb through my mop of curly hair, which left me with a present-day horror of going to a beauty salon:

"On pain of death, do not pull my hair."

She also stoked the flames of competitive jealousy among the siblings.

"At your age, your sister was already doing cartwheels."

How could I not want to kill the competition? Particularly my younger sister, Arlene, whose life began with my enmity. I took every opportunity to give her a punch, a kick, or, my favorite, a tiny bite. She gave back as good as she got.

My mother was judge and jury, anointed by divine proclamation. Like Charlton Heston atop Mount Sinai, my father dutifully proclaimed my mother's commandments. He had the voice and physique to pull it off. He was a handsome man who stood six feet tall and possessed of a thunderous basso voice. The family trembled when he used it.

From an early age, I knew that *the princes*, aka the four boys, were the preferred sex in the household, right down to their extra portions at the dinner table. Whatever talents my four brothers possessed were enthusiastically supported throughout high school and college: piano lessons, violin lessons, chemistry laboratory workshops, and model airplane workshops.

Before the Depression, no expense was spared. After the Depression, the family made do with second-hand clothes, tools, and tutus. I grew up in two families.

The first five, in order of age, Raymond, Allyn, Marilyn, Elliot, and Lucille, were born *before* the Depression. The last three, David, Sally-Jane, and Arlene, were born *after*.

The Depression took a big bite out of the family budget. My parents sacrificed to provide the best teachers and classes for their eight talented children. It was easy in New York City, which was a mecca for great teachers and free scholarship programs and special schools, many of which, in my early years, I was a beneficiary.

Boys had a fast-track ticket to a better education and continued support of their pursuits. Why? They never got pregnant. It took me years to realize that as soon as one of my sisters or I began to menstruate, our lives were redirected. Like rejected virgins from the local Vestal Temple, my mother prepared us for the marriage market. Dance, art, and music lessons were continued only to attract a husband. The more cultured and sophisticated we were, the more likely we would attract a higher-quality prospect.

My mother's form of birth control was to preach the horrors and evils of sex. She proclaimed that the sex act was the most disgusting part of being married. Narrating horror stories about how she suffered having to "do it" traumatized me. And yet... something didn't add up. My father was only the nominal head of our household. My mother was the real power. She had twelve pregnancies and eight children. That's a lot of suffering. Why didn't she just say, "*no*"? There was no way I would even think about asking her that question. Unless I wanted a mouth full of soap.

At 13, I got my period and prayed to God to take it back. My mother's terrifying admonitions fell on uneducated ears. I didn't know any of my body parts, where they were, what they did. I didn't understand how a girl got pregnant.
From a hug?
Maybe playing Post Office?

If there had been any other way to escape, I never would have married. But I was a coward. I lacked the courage to confront or rebel against my parents. I was Freud's paralyzed, hysterical girl.
If you don't believe me, ask any of the men in my life.
That might be difficult.
Most of them are dead.

6

Antecedents

My mother, Anna, was born and raised in a three-floored, many-roomed Victorian manse in Borough Park, Brooklyn, at a time when much of Brooklyn was daisy fields. The house was encircled by a gingerbread-style wrap-around porch, which, as a little girl, became the stage for many of my early theatrical productions. My grandfather, her father David, a Ukrainian immigrant from the shtetls of Kiev, was a winner in the American immigrant success story sweepstakes. He steerage classed alone over the ocean at the age of 13 and then apprenticed himself to a skilled cabinet maker.

He began his American success story by pushing his cart filled with tools, talent, and an overriding ambition from one Wall Street office to another. Over time, he created an empire of high-quality, custom-made office furniture and cabinets.

The house was originally bought for his wife, two daughters, two sons, housekeeper, cook, and assorted daily help. Unfortunately, after his wife Rachel died, an early victim of the Spanish flu, he was left in this huge house with his two daughters, two sons, housekeeper, cook, and assorted daily help and no idea how to raise children. My mother, Anna, was his oldest daughter. By tradition and her father's needs, after her mother died, she assumed the mantle of childcare and household duties. She was 16.

Along with the more common adolescent female anxieties, her mother's early death filled her with an uncommon fear of life. She dutifully shared these anxieties with her siblings. Her only sister, Edith, got the message and left the house early to marry. This left my mother and her teenage brothers, Ben and Irving, in a huge house with a housekeeper, cook, and assorted daily help.

Her widowed father, safe in the assurance of his daughter's spinsterhood, moved from the huge Brooklyn house to a suite of rooms at the Roosevelt Hotel in New York City to become a merry widower. He was a bon vivant dandy with a Ukrainian accent so thick as to render him almost incomprehensible. His accent might have prevented him from making public speeches, but not from enjoying and spending his money.

Against all odds, but then again, no one who knew her would ever bet against my mother, Anna beat the old maid rap. At 25, she met and courted Louis, an employee from her father's business. Yes, she courted him. They married in 1919.

The relationship between my mother, Anna, and my father, Louis, is another book, and I would probably die before finishing it. Here is the abridged and condensed version.

My mother was a first-generation American.
And a complete snob about that.

Her father may have had a thick Ukrainian accent, but he was rich. She was a snob about that, too.

She had servants and tutors and lived in a large mansion in Brooklyn...
a snob.

Anna was traumatized by her mother's death when she was 16. Not only because she was forced into a role she didn't ask and wasn't prepared for, but I think if there was any love in her life, it had come from her mother. Her mother's death created an emptiness within her that Anna was never able to fill. Maybe that's why she kept having children. Her need to control came with an automatic admonition whenever her children threatened that control:

25

"There is nothing worse than living with a dead mother. You are lucky. Your mother is alive."

Anna married an immigrant. She pretended she didn't.

My father's family, also from a shtetl somewhere in the Austrian-Hungary Empire, arrived in New York City in the early part of the twentieth century. They were the more typical immigrants of their era, struggling to find those streets paved in gold. By marrying Anna, Louis's birth family thought he was set for life. He was. But not always a happy one. Marrying a woman with money wasn't the cure-all it was supposed to be.

7

Little Orphan Annie and Lost Louis

M y father had always loved school. He enrolled in courses towards a degree at City College. He wanted to be an actor, which is why he hung around the vaudeville houses. As a good son, he was obliged to find a job and help with his family's expenses.

Louis searched for a job that would allow him to pursue his part-time college studies along with his theatrical dream. My rich Ukrainian grandfather was searching for a messenger for his Brooklyn furniture factory. Employee met employer, and fate, destiny, coincidence; synchronicity had a field day.

Louis was tasked with delivering a message to Anna from her father. Sending Louis with a message for Anna was like sending St. John the Baptist to deliver his head to Salome. Anna, five feet in her stockings, looked up at this delicious six-footer, established he was Jewish, and it was all over.

They married in June, and in July, Anna traveled alone to a hotel in the Catskills to recover. From what? I don't know. That has never stopped me from making it up.

From the time Louis delivered that message to Anna right through to the day of their marriage, there was bad blood between my grandfather and my father. Anna tried desperately to bring the warring parties together. Not possible then, or ever. After the honeymoon, Anna had a nervous breakdown. She went to the Catskills for a "rest cure." What the hell was going on? It's embarrassing. It's shameful. It's outrageous. And, ultimately, stupid but predictable.

My shtetl-born Ukrainian immigrant grandfather did not approve of my shtetl-born Austrian-Hungary immigrant father. His younger daughter Edith married a successful American-born businessman. Both his sons married American-born young women. He was ashamed that his American-born daughter married a foreign-born immigrant who lived in a ghetto tenement similar to the one he lived in when he first came to America.

Every time my grandfather opened his mouth to speak, he was barely understood. Every time my father opened his mouth, he sounded like the well-spoken, educated actor that he was. If it hadn't caused such havoc in my family, it would be laughable. Isn't it a shame that being foreign-born and poor makes you the target of so much anger and anguish? So what else is new?

Louis would never escape his father-in-law's charge of marrying Anna for her money. Louis hadn't realized that his desire to be an actor terrified Anna. My father was talented. But he didn't have the kind of talent necessary to sidestep Anna's manipulations. He lost control of his own life. It was probably for the best. He had a very fragile ego. He wouldn't have survived in the world of art, where rejection was a major component of an artist's life. He was comfortable with strong, assertive women like his mother, and now Anna was telling him what to do. When life didn't go his way, and much of the time it didn't, he always had someone to blame.

Shortly after Anna returned to Brooklyn from her "vapors" in the Catskills, Louis announced he was taking a job as an executive with a company in Chicago that manufactured brassieres, corsets, and girdles. Why? His father-in-law didn't live in Chicago, and he was going to prove to everyone that he could provide for himself and Anna without her money. He didn't know anything about managing or directing a business. He knew less than nothing about brassieres, girdles, or corsets. But he was an actor, and for the rest of his life, he acted like he knew what he was doing. Sometimes it worked. Most of the time, it didn't.

8

Parental Love

My parent's blend of fears and anxieties found satisfaction in the raising and disciplining of their children.

Later, at annual family meetings, while my parents were alive, my siblings and I would gather and laugh as we recalled the crimes and the punishments meted out to us when we were children.

I remember when I was seven or eight, I was caught telling a lie. Since I always lied, I don't remember what it was about.

Louis: "Sally-Jane! It is a sin to tell a lie."

He was so emphatic and dramatic that I almost believed him. But, he always lied too, about paying the bills, his life in the theatre, his success as a businessman. I pretended I believed him because I didn't want to be punished. It didn't matter. My mother still held me by my arms and gave me a couple of deep pinches – one for each arm. They really hurt. Better a pinch than a comb-through on my curly-headed mop of hair. That pain was excruciating. My eyes teared for hours.

I'd like to excuse and forgive my parents' version of discipline. I can't. I don't care if it was the norm for the era... *spare the rod, spoil the child*. Their personal failures and frustrations stoked the fire of their physical punishments. How can someone so much bigger physically abuse someone so much smaller? It didn't make sense to me then. It doesn't make sense to me now. Here's the clincher. This is done in the name of *love*? Is it any wonder why that word causes such perversion in the world?

I love you. WHACK!
I love you. WHAM!

However, Anna had other maternal qualities. Depending on the talent and inclinations of her eight different children, she came up with eight different programs of study. She took each of us by the hand to our first classes. She encouraged our progress. She was amazing. Her energy exhausted all of us. Today, she'd be considered CEO material. Her contradictory behavior confused the hell out of me. She nurtured my gifts. But at the same time, she was this angry, overbearing, volatile screamer, pincher, hair puller. At least she broadcast her mood changes. Not Louis. Just like your classic passive-aggressive, you never knew when he would explode.

Anna's only weapon in a fight with Louis was her father's money. So humiliating. When my father wasn't angry, he was very good at smoking cigars, telling jokes, playing the violin, singing, and, like a judge, handing down Anna's decisions. None of this eased the pain at his inability to pay any share of the family's expenses. His salary was limited to sweet treats and Coney Island hot dogs. His judgemental father-in-law considered him a failure and a sponge. His wife, on the one hand, defended him and, on the other hand, defeated him.

When his anger and frustration over his life choices hit a boiling point, his belt would slip off, signaling that no good would ever come from that gesture.

I think the reason Anna had so many children was to keep Louis from running away to that circus in his mind.

If you were born into the Heit family, you had to be "special," a child prodigy. Anna and Louis needed to have special children. Their intimidation and pressure to succeed applied to all of us. The children who just wanted to *be* and not constantly have to prove they were special because they weren't, fell under the bus. Until I was three, I thought I was the most special of all my brothers and sisters. I knew I was destined to be a star.

9

Every Night A Little Death

(Thank you, Stephen Sondheim)

I lived in an enchanted house in Brooklyn that held my dreams of stardom along with my parents' rabbitual habit of birthing children. To the left of a grand hallway, French doors led into the living and music rooms. It was called the music room because it held a beautiful Knabe baby grand player piano, my father and brothers' violins, the triangles the little ones played, and a large mahogany cabinet where books, sheets of music, and player rolls for the piano, overflowed from every shelf. I owned this room because it was my stage. I was my sisters' and brothers' three-year-old curly-haired, tiny, towheaded version of Shirley Temple.

My mother was going to have another baby. I wasn't worried. At three, I was adorable and talented. My place in the family was safe and secure. Or so I thought.

A three-year-old doesn't have much of a memory. My brother David, at five, didn't have much more. Between the two of us, we were able to piece together much of the puzzlement of our abandonment.

One minute, I was in my enchanted house with adoring brothers, sisters, mother, father, and the next moment someone waved an evil magic wand. It was all gone—except for David.

David and I have no memory of our father driving us to Uncle Irving and Aunt Miriam's house (my mother's brother and his wife) in White Plains in our family's 1936 Studebaker. Without explanation, we were left there, suspended with no ground beneath our feet. No matter what good intentions they might have had, my aunt, uncle, and father's silence was selfish, destructive, and cruel. Our time of terror began.

I spent the next three months waiting, waiting for my father to remember where he left two of his children. Any minute, he would return David and me to our lost mother and family. Every time a door opened or someone walked upstairs, I thought, *Daddy's here.*

We had been driven away to a strange house inhabited by strangers. What had we done? It was obvious. I had done something terrible. I was so glad that David had done something terrible, too. Oh God, I was so grateful he was a bad boy. I wasn't alone. I clung to him. Without him, I didn't exist. I was never going to let him go.

Aunt Miriam and Uncle Irving had two children the same ages as David and me. Their house was big enough for all of us. It should have worked. It didn't.

The household was brilliantly organized. Every day was so quiet you could hear a pin drop. There was no music.

My parents' household was brilliantly disorganized. Every day was a seven-ring circus. If nothing else, the Heits loved music. Someone was always playing the piano, the violin, singing, dancing... a circus.

Miriam and Irving observed holidays but didn't celebrate them.

My family celebrated everything. Your tooth came out – there was meatloaf with a candle.

The only Jewish holiday Miriam and Irving observed was Hanukkah. What kind of a Jew was that?

At home, we celebrated Hanukkah and Christmas. Louis was the best Jewish Santa Claus. There probably was none before him, and I have never heard of another since. After sitting on his lap and telling him what I wanted, Mrs. Claus would lead me to my pile of presents. Oh, Glory!

Thanksgiving dinner at Miriam and Irving's was in a very formal dining room with a very formal table setting. Which spoon? Which fork? Servings were apportioned on your plate and handed around to each of us by the maid.

Thanksgiving dinner at home was messy, with a groaning table of food, food, and more food. Our manners were more aligned with a logging camp than a house in White Plains. We were used to a noisy table of children passing and heaping preferred foods onto their plates while sneaking unpreferred foods onto someone else's plate. It wasn't unusual to have a food fight when a brother or sister found his or her plate filled with succotash or over-fried fish. I think my mother purposely over-fried the fish so we wouldn't know it wasn't fresh.

If food and holidays were the only differences, it still might have worked. While Anna's child-rearing was stuck in the Victorian era, Miriam adhered to the latest how-to books. With eight children, by sheer necessity, Anna adopted a Victorian laissez-faire. She couldn't be in seven different places at seven different times with seven different children. This meant there were certain childhood training habits that Anna ignored: wait for everyone to be served before eating, do not speak until spoken to, eat with your mouth closed, use a napkin instead of your sleeve, and, most importantly to me and David, she never checked her own children's bowel movements.

Miriam, like the feminine version of an Army drill Sergeant that she was, followed all these training habits and so much more. She actually charted our individual movements. If David or I missed a day, the dreaded enema was unhooked and made ready. I am pretty sure my gastric system was permanently affected by her routine plumbing schedule. I am also sure that just the unhooking of the enema stopped any movement that might have been.

We slept in the attic. I never understood why. Later, I thought about it and realized she probably didn't want her children contaminated by those undisciplined Heits.

It was 1936, the height of the Depression. Irving worked for his rich father, and there was money. My father was a salaried employee, and there was no money. The contrast between the two households made our stay more uncomfortable and painful. To David and me, Aunt Miriam and Uncle Irving's house was a foreign country.

We were beginning to understand that we had been abandoned by our family and, now, for whatever reason, were also separated from the family we were living with. It was obvious. No one wanted us because we had done something unspeakable.

My three-year-old brain finally figured out how this whole thing happened. The night before everything I knew disappeared, I had closed my eyes. That was it. As long as I was at Aunt Miriam and Uncle Irving's house, I would never close my eyes. If I did, the next thing to disappear would be me. Every night was a battle to stay awake. To keep my eyes open. Every morning, when I realized I had not disappeared, I convinced myself it was because I hadn't closed my eyes. To this day, the slightest anxiety about almost anything gives me an open-eyed all-nighter.

I don't remember who or when, but years later, someone explained to me that my mother had had a stroke, a total loss of speech and movement. She went into labor. My father took her to the hospital, where she delivered her eighth child, my sister Arlene. For the next three months, my mother remained in the hospital in rehabilitation and recovery – paid for by her father, of course.

Eventually, Arlene was brought home with a baby nurse. When my father returned to work, my grandfather hired a housekeeper to oversee the house and my five older siblings, who were already in school.

If we were to stay at home, David and I would have needed supervision. The house was already full to bursting. Louis was already accepting money from his nemesis. He wouldn't accept another penny. Another nurse was financially out of the question. Miriam and Irving volunteered to take care of us until my mother recovered.

I blamed both my mother and my father for the banishment. How stupid is that? Anna was literally and figuratively "out of it." This is not to say she wouldn't have concurred with everyone's decision about the situation. I don't know.

I do know I created a special inner compartment where, whenever necessary, I could hate her with impunity. It took forever to see that hate was a cover for how much I loved and missed her. Life is just not fair.

10

The Aftermath

I don't remember arriving home. I am sure my father drove to Miriam and Irving's house in the Studebaker to pick us up and return us home. I have no memory of that. Maybe I didn't think it was real. I don't know.

When we arrived home, the nurse was there with my baby sister. My mother was still rehabilitating at the hospital. I felt an immediate hatred for Arlene and her nurse. They were in my house. My mother wasn't. I was happy to blame them for all my misery. Whoever said feelings are rational doesn't know what they're talking about.

After this trauma, I led a brilliantly duplicitous life. I either growled or grinned, depending on what was most advantageous. When I was called upon to entertain, I still relied on *This Is Pinky*, but as I grew older, I added safety songs to my repertoire:

Remember your name and address
And telephone number too.
Then, if someday you lose your way
You'll know just what to do

My world had changed. At any moment, someone, anyone, could put me in a car and drive me away from my life. I needed to protect myself. From the time of my return until not so long ago, I didn't always believe what anyone said or did. I was done with trusting.

Years later, when I was eight or nine, I claimed the side porch as my private theatre. The windows were low to the porch level and high almost to the ceiling, which made perfect exits and entrances for the plays I wrote. I gathered the cast from neighbors, school friends, and, on special occasions, David, who always played my Prince Charming. My cast of characters were the usual suspects: the king, the jester, the hero/prince, and the ugly stepsisters (I had three). I always played the lead, the princess or the queen.

For one of my plays, I needed a princess costume. Lucille had just bought a beautiful evening dress for her prom. The skirt was made with yards and yards of puffy white tulle... perfect Princess costume. The top of the dress didn't fit my eight-year-old figure. I cut it off.

Lucille's response was predictable. She beat me black and blue. And then she cursed me.

"Before you went to Miriam and Irving's house, you were nice. Now, you are an angry, nasty pain in the neck. No one likes you. Especially now. I hope the next time Daddy takes you away he never brings you back. I hate you."

I didn't fit into the family anymore. I trusted no one but David. He handled his re-entry differently. He attached himself to brother Elliot, becoming his stooge. Elliot was his protector and defense against another life storm.

I'd like to be able to tell you that with years of trauma therapy and weekend workshops in rebirthing to open memory blockages, I recovered my original mojo, but I can't. In truth, I never recovered. I still have trust issues. Never quite sure if I believe anyone. Oh, sure, I was psychoanalyzed to within an inch of my life, and I can psychobabble with the best of them about the reasons for my devious, deceitful years, but I have to admit it doesn't take much to feed into my fear of abandonment.

The fear of disappearance, aka death, is a constant in my life. From childhood to aging adulthood, reality has brought a soupcon of intellectual acceptance of death and only the beginning of a spiritual surrender.

Let's leave it at that for now. I'd like to get back to the story so I can find out what happened.

11

Poor Relations

A nna and Louis needed to feel that each of their children, Raymond, Allyn, Marilyn, Elliot, Lucille, David, Sally-Jane, and Arlene, were special even if they couldn't remember their names.

Anna: "Allyn, no, Elliot, uh, I mean Raymond, no, David...????"
One of us would always answer, "Charlie, Mom. My name is Charlie!"

The Heit House Orchestra had no shortage of triangle players. All eight of us had one piano teacher, Augusta Kahn. She would come to the house in Brooklyn. She began the lessons with the oldest three, and by the time she got to the youngest three, she was fried... "Have a triangle!"

There was a great benefit to being the seventh of eight children. By the time she got to me, Anna was exhausted. My mother was still strong enough to move the mountain of any small child's opposition. However, if I stayed out of her sight, she would forget about me and my crimes. I was able to get away with murder. I operated on the axiom of what she didn't know wouldn't hurt me. I was a sneaky and devious kid, seconds away from a life of crime.

Living in the environs of New York City, my passion to perform saved me. I was very busy – regular school and after-school lessons in drama, dance, and music. Neighborhood Playhouse, an actor's conservatory before the Actor's Studio, had a Saturday children's program with the best teachers. Martha Graham and her company for movement, the best voice and diction technicians. I almost lost my Brooklyn/New York accent... almost.

My mother operated in a world of paradoxes and contradictions. On the one hand, she recognized my talent and was ready to play Mama Rose to my baby Sally-Jane. She was also adamant that I go to college in case my husband, whomever she anointed, lost his job. This rule was written during the Depression when Louis lost his business.

Yet, the possibility that I could succeed terrified her. Her terror was antithetical to all the care she took to train my talent. Then, again, logic was never her strong suit.

Much of my mother's and father's life was hidden. None of us had any idea where they had the sex to produce eight children. Six of them were in close proximity to their bedroom. No one ever heard a sound. They must have done it outside. Maybe in the cherry tree? They waited until the wee hours of the morning when we were all in deep sleep? Clearly, they found the time and the place. I was no dummy. Of course, you couldn't hear them. The stork had brought trouble and my baby sister, Arlene.

None of us knew how they fed and clothed us. There were a few indications. All my clothes were well worn by my sisters before me: *Second Hand Sally*. A couple of times a year, on Jewish High Holy Days and my birthday, I was gifted a new coat, a pair of shoes, and a new dress–not all at the same time: birthdays, the coat, Holy Days, the shoes, and the dress for Temple.

How did they do it? How were they able to provide food and sustenance for all eight of us? The city provided scholarship programs in various subjects for the soul. Her rich father provided for the body.

Money talk was a no-no and relegated to the future of a future son or daughter-in-law. Somehow, we children knew not to ask for what we surely wouldn't get unless it was a dire necessity. Those dire necessities–Bar Mitzvahs, weddings, tuition, medical bills, mortgage, and utilities–were the cause of much pain for my mother.

I discovered only later how often, with her tail between her legs, she was forced to beg for money from her father. Either my younger sister Arlene or I accompanied her. Our presence deflected the slings and arrows my grandfather hurled at his only daughter to embarrass and shame her. It had to be either one of us. Anyone older would have known what was really happening.

My grandfather thought my mother and father were irresponsible. No viable means of support, *and* they kept having children. What was wrong with them?
They were Jewish.
Not Catholic.

We would take the subway from Brooklyn to his office in the Chrysler Building, an impressive fortress with its exotic and fearful gargoyles, art deco design, and marble floors. King David granted us an audience in his Chrysler Castle. After much bowing and scraping, my grandfather granted my mother money for those dire necessities.

I didn't know what was going on. And yet, in the way that children *know* without being told, I knew my mother was unhappy, uncomfortable, and in a lot of pain. She was one person going into his office. Her shame and embarrassment walked in before her. She was the same person when she left his office. Her shame and embarrassment walked out after her.

I never understood why my mother didn't ask me to perform for him. Even then, I had enough hubris to think one song would fix everything for everyone. Don't ask me why or how. I just know that it happened in every Betty Grable movie I ever saw, so why not in my grandfather's office?

12

A Star Step

I couldn't keep up with the mood swings of my mother. One minute, I was to prepare myself for the misfortunes of marriage. The next, I was preparing auditions for a new high school for the performing arts. Without discussing it with me, she went to the Board of Education in Manhattan and filled out an audition application in my name for both the Dance and Drama Departments at the new school.

Did she want me to be a star or not? It was crazy-making. On the chance she was onto something, I happily followed my mother's orders. I prepared a monologue for my drama audition, a recitation of *The Highwayman* by Alfred Noyes, which I had learned in my Saturday elocution classes:

The wind was a torrent of darkness among the gusty trees
The Moon was a ghostly galleon tossed upon cloudy seas
The road was a ribbon of moonlight over the purple moor
And the highwayman came riding - riding - riding
The Highwayman came riding up to the old inn door.

So spooky. I brought just the right amount of mystery and movement to my recitation. My gestures were infused with a combination of my favorite horror movie heroes, Boris Karloff and Bela Lugosi. Years of speech lessons coupled with the necessity of being heard over the crowd at home gave me a big voice able to startle my audience. I thought I was brilliant.

Martha Graham, *the* Martha Graham, was there for my dance audition. I had no shame. My first selection was the Boston Pops Orchestral recording of *Bolero*. I tangoed around the room violently, making silent film screen gestures of a woman losing her mind. I wonder what an analyst would say about every dance I ever choreographed, which was always about someone going crazy. Before Martha could stop me, I put on my second choice—a recording of Johannes Strauss's *Blue Danube Waltz*. Pretending I was costumed in a hoop skirt over many crinolines, swirling, dipping, turning, and being coyly flirtatious, I spun around the room. I just knew she was watching a star being born. The fact that Martha Graham didn't leave immediately after or even before I finished was either because she was a glutton for punishment or she arrived at the auditions pre-medicated.

Shock of shocks. I was accepted in both departments.

The battle wasn't over. The principal of the high school where I was pre-registered balked. Too much bureaucratic paperwork to redo my application for the new school. He refused to send over my records to Performing Arts. Anna was livid. I am beyond grateful that I wasn't there. She marched over to the old high school. Many blocks away from our house. Unannounced, without knocking, walked right into the Principal's office:

"How dare you! My daughter is a star. She was born to go to this school. She is an American. It's in the Constitution. Of the people, by the people, and for the people... her right to her pursuit of happiness... You can't prevent her from attending the new school. I...I... I will report you to the truant officer."

This five-foot, straggly hair-tucked-into-an-unkempt bun, plump woman in a frock little more than a housedress successfully cowed the Principal. The records were sent.

I was accepted into the first class ever of the High School of Performing Arts. My mother chose the drama program over the dance program. Actors had a longer shelf life. She was a housewife and a mother, not a producer, but she knew everything. Actors, directors, dancers, and musicians of great repute and experience were our teachers. The classes were small, the competition intense; it all felt familiar to me.

You would think classes filled with young boys and girls with oversized egos and of all shapes and colors would make it impossible to find a friend. It was. In the Drama Department, I made friends mostly with the boys. Back then, there was no such thing as gender fluidity, so having a male friend provided no competition for a female role. Conard was my high school crush who, because of my fear of sex, became my best "male pal friend." What a waste. He was so adorable.

My best friend Ellen was a dance major. Dancers didn't audition for Drama Department plays... no competition there. Ellen betrayed our friendship by leaving school to marry a man she met during a family vacation. I wanted to punish her, but when she made me a bridesmaid, I couldn't. All I could think of was that she was going to do that disgusting thing my mother warned me that married couples had to do. I felt sorry for her. Also, I didn't understand how she could want a husband more than wanting to be a star.

Before the school got its own building near Lincoln Center, we were housed in an old abandoned school on 46th Street between Broadway and 6th Avenue (Avenue of the Americas). The siren song of Broadway that I and many of my fellow students heard most of the time was just around the corner.

I had another good friend, Ron, a male dance major who years later became a very successful Broadway choreographer/director. While in high school we would sneak out of school on Wednesday matinee days to catch a show. We couldn't pay. We waited until the intermission and mingled with the ticketed crowds. When they returned to their seats we followed them into the theatre and waited to find an empty seat. We justified it as an acting exercise. We were good. We never got caught.

I can't say during my years at Performing Arts that I did much performing. I spent my lunchtime in the cafeteria dancing like a fool to the Big Bands and the beginning of Rock and Roll music. It was blasted through speakers set up by students and faculty. I think someone had this brilliant idea that the incredible neurotic, nervous energy of artistic, temperamental teenagers like myself got a real workout and made the afternoon easier for the faculty. I don't remember ever sitting down and eating my lunch. I was always dancing.

In my last year of high school, I wasn't cast in many plays. Sidney Lumet, my drama teacher, was a method man. This is an acting technique that asks you to go deep inside to find an experience within yourself that helps you understand and relate to the character you play. At that time in my life there was no way I was able to go deep inside anywhere. The darkness of my early childhood forbade that journey. You can spot the difference between a method and a non-method actor. In method acting, the actor, by the depth of his or her characterization, gives the audience an opportunity to see the inner workings of the character he or she is playing, allowing the audience to identify with that character and, even if it's a villain, have empathetic feelings. A really good method actor can alter your perception of Iago. He will never be blameless, but he can be understood. This is the core of an actor's work. Give your character dimension, truth. You think the concept and words are too much for a 17-year-old? Not! I understood it. I just couldn't achieve it. I saw how classmates with less talent could go within and pull out a truthful character. I went within and pulled out... nothing.

He cast me in only one show. I played an outrageous, farcical character. I didn't have to go inside. I could strut the stage, say my lines, and make the audience laugh. I was funny. The die was cast.

I did really good classwork with other teachers and fellow classmates. I learned a great deal and made a few forever friends.

I'm not sure. Maybe it was while I was in Performing Arts that I discovered that no matter how many times I was asked to dance at lunchtime jive sessions or how many laughs my character pulled from the audience, something was missing. I had no idea what it was. I just knew I didn't have it.

Now, that is definitely beyond a 17-year-old's comprehension.

13

Nobody Asked Me

O f course, no one asked me, but when my grandfather sold the old Brooklyn house where my mother was born, it changed everything for everyone.

It all began with World War II when the house emptied as my three older brothers, Raymond, Allyn, and Elliot, enlisted in the Army, Navy, and Army Air Corps. My oldest sister married her World War II Army officer beau. You didn't need a microscope to see that the glue that held the house and family together was drying up as the family was breaking up. Only four of us were to be left in this big house with three floors, each with as many rooms all going to rot and ruin. It looked like a decaying haunted house occupied by Boris and Bela.

My grandfather had purchased it for his family at the end of the 19th Century. Since 1919, it had been worn down by the actions and habits of eight wild children. My mother was hard-pressed to keep her eyes on all of us. Each of us in our time did as much damage as we could. Anna and Louis had no money for repairs and absolutely none for improvements. Every winter month, coal was delivered through the special coal shuttle window into the cellar. Every night, my father went down into the cellar and shoveled enough coal into the old furnace to keep our bodies warm. Well, not every night. Sometimes, my grandfather forgot to order the coal. Yes, that successful, rich, thick-accented Ukrainian immigrant still blamed my mother for marrying an unsuccessful, poor immigrant. Pop added another grievance.

"Anna, so many children. Why? You're not a shiksa (non-Jew), you're Jewish."

No one understood, even Anna. Anna's children were her raison d'etre.

Raymond was Anna and Louis' first star in the firmament of their family-pride-filled galaxy. At 17, he sold and designed several model airplanes, which are manufactured to this day. Before Raymond left for his battle with our enemies, he made an enemy of our mother. He eloped with his girlfriend, Shirley. Anna lost control of Raymond to Shirley and her family. She never forgave either of them. Black mark.

Allyn, a genius chemist, was on the autism spectrum before anyone knew there was an autism spectrum and was plagued by mental illness. He spent much of the war years in St. Elizabeth's Hospital in Washington, D.C., where Ezra Pound was also committed. Anna and Louis, products of their time, were embarrassed and ashamed. Black mark.

Marilyn, the oldest sister, aka Sis, didn't stand a chance against Anna's stubborn iron-fisted control. Sis's dreams of the theatre, acting, and dancing were squished and squashed. She took the only escape route available to women of her era and married Sam, an army officer headed to North Africa. Mom never forgave Marilyn for falling in love with Sam, who was born into a poor immigrant family from Romania.

Anna to Marilyn: "All men from Romania are horse thieves. You are cursed."

I am pretty sure she made that up so she could punish Marilyn. Anna was her father's daughter. Anna's daughter was doing exactly what she had done all those years ago. She was marrying beneath her.

Damn Voltaire and his smarts... *History doesn't repeat itself; people do.*

In keeping with Anna's mood swings and contradictory behavior, she gave her daughter Marilyn and Sam a brilliant wedding. The old homestead was converted into a cornucopia of trays of glorious food, with beautiful flowers everywhere, all of it accompanied by beautiful music. Growing up, Marilyn had constantly challenged Anna's control. After she married, she continued to challenge that control. That was a no-no. Black mark.

Elliot, the last of the World War II brothers, enlisted in the Army Air Corps and trained as a pilot. After the war, he desperately wanted to attend West Point. One of Louis's major successes in the lore of family life is the years he spent working and cajoling Brooklyn politicians to give Elliot an appointment to the Point. He succeeded. Elliot's nickname at West Point was Stud. He became a jet pilot and married a lovely woman from a very wealthy family. He had NO BLACK MARK!

Lucille was the artist of the family. She went to a special art high school and studied design at the Fashion Institute of Technology. When she moved out of the old Brooklyn house into the Westchester house she was a successful fashion illustrator. She fell afoul of Anna and Louis because she became seriously involved with a wannabe opera singer who was not Jewish. The family battles that ensued from this relationship shook the foundations of the house and of Lucille's heart and mind. She threatened to kill herself. Anna and Louis backed down but not out. Lucille married Ed. Anna, like a judge in a British melodrama, placed a black triangular cloth atop her head. Lucille was condemned. She tried desperately to return to Anna's favor and prostrated herself before her mother, begging to be forgiven. Without apologizing for her marriage, she apologized for her marriage. In every way, she was begging Anna, *Mommy, control me.* And, of course, Anna did as she was bid. She still never forgave her. Black mark.

David was a people pleaser, very like our father. He inhaled failure like it was mother's milk. But David was my cellmate at Aunt Miriam and Uncle Irving's house when we were little so we are bonded through eternity. No matter what, I shall always be there for him. David wanted to be an actor. I think my father thought if he couldn't be an actor no one could. Anna and Louis needed someone to be a doctor in the family. David would have made a good doctor if he hadn't flunked out of medical school. He would have played a brilliant Willy Loman in Death of a

Salesman because he was Willy Loman. He ended up measuring and selling uniforms. Black mark.

I never felt part of the family. They had already done their worst to me, so I didn't care. As a child, I was headed for reformatory school, anyway. I was a first-class liar. When my father was in the bathroom, I crept into his bedroom, went into the pockets of his pants, and stole any loose change that was in there. My little dance case was always on the ready. Packed with my leotard, ballet slippers, and Twinkies. At least once a month, I ran away from home. In my heart, I waited in vain for them to send out search parties with special search dogs to find me, and when they did, tearfully in relief, they hugged and kissed me and weren't angry at all. Running away was a major theme in my life. What a doofus I was. I ran away from the good as well as the bad. The way I look at it, I probably had the most black marks in the family.

The baby of the family, Arlene, followed the straight and narrow path of parental favor and approval. She did what was expected of her, and she did it well. She married her Ronnie, showing most of us in unhappy marriages what a happy marriage looked like. Arlene remained the baby and a favorite of the family, which bothered me for most of my life until it didn't and doesn't.

It was amazing. Elliot and Arlene were the only two of the eight children with no black marks. Anna and Louis swore they never had favorites, but every time they swore, their noses grew.

14

Leaving Brooklyn

T he neighborhood had changed from a sweet, pastoral selection of large single-family homes in a daisy field to a street packed with closely built multiple-family dwellings. My rich grandfather was embarrassed that his only daughter lived in what he called a ghetto. He refused to visit.

"Anna! I sold the house. Are you going to live on the street or in the house I bought for you in Westchester?"

My father was not consulted. If it involved big money like mortgages and utilities, he was never consulted. We children always knew when Pop made a financial decision without Louis's consent. His mood went dark. If you were smart you stayed out of his way. Louis couldn't have afforded any contribution. His salary was barely enough to cover food and his commute to the office. My grandfather paid the bulk of the family's expenses. What more could Anna and Pop do to Louis's already bruised ego and pride?

I was finishing my sophomore year at the High School of Performing Arts. I moved out of NYC and into the new house in Westchester County. I missed the old house. It's where I left my dreams and fantasies.

I hated sharing a bedroom with my sister, Arlene. Her birth, the cause of my greatest childhood trauma, was bad enough, but she was also the baby of the family and held my parent's attention the longest. It wasn't fair. I was the star.

The house in Westchester had four bedrooms. One for myself and Arlene, one for David, one for Lucille, and one for Anna and Louis.

For my mother, the move to the suburbs was the most traumatic. Her security, the home she was born in, decayed and dilapidated as it was, disappeared, and with it went her safety net. In defiance, she bought a small spinet piano for private use in her bedroom. If you couldn't find her, you could hear her. She was consorting with Brahms, Chopin, Mozart in the privacy of her boudoir. Tensions released and relieved, she re-entered ready to engage with her children and her life.

Initially, I was excited to attend a new high school because I was playing a new part. The Mickey Rooney, Judy Garland high school movie musicals prepared me for my next starring role. I convinced my mother to buy the requisite saddle shoes.

The school was a beautiful ivy-covered building in a campus setting. A far cry from the aged run-down schools of NYC. It looked like the movie set of Good News with fraternities, sororities, et al. I was "rushed." I was chosen. I was thrilled. One of my pledge requirements was to read and memorize the sorority's constitution. In bold print, I read:

No Jews allowed.

Whoa!

I was a Jew. A Reform Jew. But a Jew. All religions are born to confuse. In Judaism, I know of three main divisions: Orthodox, Conservative, Reform. Each sect was a little less strict with the rules and traditions of the one before it. A Reform Jew was as close as you could get to being a Christian without being baptized. When I was seven, I was so jealous when my best friend Catherine had her First Communion. I wanted her bridal dress, white stockings, white shoes, and most of all, the little paper beribboned basket of white almonds the priest gave her.

As a reform Jew, I was confirmed in my temple's Sunday School. No big deal. In 1948, before Betty Friedan et al., girls did not have a Bat Mitzvah. We were a family that took our Reform Judaism seriously. We celebrated Christmas as well as Hanukkah. My father, frustrated actor that he was, played a brilliant Santa Claus. I remember along the way of many celebrations, he lost his Santa suit. He still had the mask. No suit. He wore a fabulous Chinese embroidered robe below his Santa hat, mask, and beard. Paired with the robe and the mask, his Santa had a decidedly oriental look. The younger ones, like myself and Arlene and, later on, grandchildren, screamed in terror when he picked us up to sit on his lap. It was clear to me a Santa who didn't look Chinese was fake.

When I read that in the sorority's constitution, I went to the president of the sorority.

"I am Jewish."

Like Munich in 1923, they held a meeting. It was decided I would be an exception. One of them actually said it would be alright because I didn't look Jewish. I didn't feel exceptional. I felt... unwell.

I am not sure, but I think, maybe for the first time, I was beginning to understand that being different wasn't just about being special and gifted.

In Brooklyn, my neighborhood was mixed: Italians, Jews, and Irish. Unidentified. In New York schools, the students were of every stripe and color. In Westchester as in most places in the late 1940s, if you were different and you could hide it, you did.

I didn't want to hide it. I didn't want to be where I wasn't wanted. I had enough of that at home.

I reapplied to the High School of Performing Arts. I gave my saddle shoes to my sister and never looked back.

I commuted via the New York, New Haven, and Hartford Railroad every day, forty-five minutes each way, for a year and a half until I graduated in 1950. Mornings, I sat amongst the busy, buzzing Westchester commuters as they read their newspapers, painted their nails, and applied their make-up, while I read plays and memorized lines. At the end of the day, I sat staring from my train window into the void, going over the credits and debits of my day. The funny, gossipy exchanges of slights, slurs, and the desperately needed attention I craved. There were so many comedians in my class, all striving for that same attention. I would choose one joke I had heard to share with my mother. While she was at the sink preparing dinner, I would regale her with the best of the jokes.

A guy goes to the doctor, and the doctor says, 'You're dying.'
The guy says, 'I want a second opinion'.
Doctor says, 'Okay, you're ugly, too!'

After a long, exhausting chore filled day, she gave me her full attention. It was a distraction for her. It was a magical time for me.

15

Reality Check

I did not want to go to college.
My parents insisted I go to college.

I said, "No."
They said, "Yes."
I said, "No."
They said, "OK."
I said, "Hooray!"
They said, "But you can never come home."

It's a conundrum. I wanted to escape. I never wanted to go home. I was afraid. I did not have the courage of my convictions. I could speak the speech but only to a mirror inside a closet.

I wanted to do what so many of my schoolmates did upon graduation from Performing Arts. I wanted to audition, professional auditions for professional productions. My wannabe friends were out there being seen. I wanted to be seen, too. Instead, I was auditioning and getting parts in college productions. It's not the same thing. If I didn't become a Star, it was always going to be the fault of my bourgeois, controlling parents, mostly my mother.

I entered Hunter College. Plan B went into effect. Now I had to find someone to rescue me by marriage... then stardom.

I knew if, anytime before a marriage, some producer, director, or agent offered me a chance, "my big Star break," whatever promises I made to whatever candidate I chose was going to be null and void.

Was I deceitful? Yes! "
Was I sorry? No!

I auditioned a lot of guys. Unfortunately, most of them were into numbers: How many girls could they persuade to go all the way? Count me out! Disgusting! I had a more important agenda. Someone had to chill their lust and accept my lust for stardom. I had no problem faking and teasing to get what I wanted. I considered it part of the price I was willing to pay to be a star.

I did find an almost. He was an almost because of his last name...
Ludvig Gesund.
Sally-Jane Heit.
The couple who gave you a blessing every time you sneezed.

Then, in the summer of my freshman year, I met Bill, the life-sized Adonis lifeguard at the local pool. At 18, he was my first teenage crush, and I did everything to attract his attention. The lifeguard chair was near the water fountain. I made so many trips to the water fountain he must have thought I had a problem.

"Could you tell me where the water fountain is?"
"In front of you."
"Silly me. When I'm on stage, I can't even see the audience."
"You're an actress?"
"Yes!"
"Can I have your..."
"I don't do autographs. It's so... so... flambé!"
"I wanted to ask for your phone number."

I thought I had died and gone to heaven. I always knew I was a good actress, but to have made such a conquest in such a short time. I was amazing.

Making one more pass to the water fountain before I left, Bill the Hunk leaned down from his chair to remind me I'd be getting a phone call from his best friend, Richard.

'If it works out, maybe we can all go on a double date with my fiance."

I tried to smile and be nonchalant; that was always an acting class challenge for me. I gave him my best Bette Davis cynical laugh.

"Ha! Ha! We'll see!"

How could he lead me on like that? His friend better not call.

I was sure he was going to be just one more guy I'd have to bat away with my increasingly absurd list of excuses as soon as a date even dared to try for first base. Not that I had any actual clue what "first base" was.

I really like you, but I feel nauseous.
I really like you, but I need to see my doctor first.
I really like you. Did you know my mother carries a gun?

The point is there was only one guy who was ever going to get to first base – the one and only one who was going to rescue me and take me away from a family who didn't love me and had no idea how talented I was.

Adonis Bill's best friend, Richard, called and introduced himself by announcing his credentials: Princeton graduate, deferred Yale Law School student. Did he think I was an employment agency? I was preparing to hang up when he suggested going to Coney Island, one of my most favorite places in the world. It's a terrible thing to admit, but I could be had for a Nathan's hot dog and a knish.

At the appointed day and hour, someone in a Rommel's open-air desert truck pulled up in front of my house.

"If that's my date," I told Mom, "I'm not home. I'd rather die than be seen in that thing."

Ignoring me, she politely opened the door to Richard's ring. I was so mortified I barely looked at him.

Thank goodness I had a scarf to keep my hair from flying off my head and to hide my face from passing cars. We made light conversation. It had to be light. Who could hear? The roar of the open-air truck engine made conversation impossible. I was all right with no talking because I was dreaming of our Coney Island destination.

Living in Brooklyn from birth to 14 years, Coney Island was a familiar haunt. As I wrote before, while my father was in the bathroom, I would steal whatever loose change I found in his pants pockets. When I had enough money – maybe a dollar or two – I would get on my bicycle and pedal from my house in Borough Park to Ocean Parkway, then ride out to Coney Island. It took about an hour. My mother was Mother Goose, who had so many children she never knew where we were...until dinner time. I made these excursions usually on a Saturday after dance class or Sunday after Sunday school. I had enough to buy a ticket on the Cyclone or the Whip, accompanied by a Nathan's hot dog or potato knish and orange drink. If I succeeded in breaking the bank of my father's pants pockets, I splurged on a luxurious paper cone of cotton candy.

I knew immediately when Richard's truck entered Coney Island. My nostrils filled with the mixed aroma of salt air, sizzling hot dogs, sauerkraut, and sweet cotton candy. Heaven. I had arrived in heaven.

Richard pulled into a parking lot near my favorite rides. As I attempted to put hair and clothes back together, I studied Richard for the first time. Not bad looking. He was tall, just under six feet. This was very important. I was five-foot-seven. It was essential that he be taller than me. Five-nine wasn't good enough. On dates, I wore three-inch heels. It would be a disaster. An absolute disaster!

His sandy hair was fashioned in a crew cut in preparation for a two-year R.O.T.C. Army stint starting in September. He was fit. He had been a lifeguard at the local pool the year before, which is where he met Bill. I was about to do further study when he began an argument with the owner of the parking lot. The owner wanted to charge Richard for two spaces. He was right; the monster truck took up two regular car spaces.

That evening, in anticipation of his future career as a lawyer, Richard argued his first case.

Richard: "It is only one vehicle."
Owner: "But it takes up two spaces."
Richard: "You don't advertise one space for one vehicle."
Owner: "I don't have to. Your whatever kind of Army truck that is takes up two spaces."
Richard: "It is only one vehicle."

My passion to perform made me different from other girls of the '50s. And yet, in so many ways, I was a typical teenager. I was mortified. I wanted the ground to open up and take me. How did I get stuck with someone arguing about spaces for a truck that belonged in a World War II movie?

I acted as though I wasn't with him. He finally agreed to pay for one and a half spaces instead of two.
He won his first case. And lost the girl.
Or so I thought...

Years after we married, he joked about the moment he fell in love with me. Walking through the Steeplechase there was a horrible freaky clown who chased girls in skirts and dresses over to underground air holes that blew their skirts up, showing their underwear. I got caught. Up went my dress. Richard fell in love. Ugh!

My indifference to Richard turned to interest in riding the Wonder Wheel, a Ferris wheel like no other. After an evening fraught with humiliation after humiliation, the Wonder Wheel earned its name and restored a silly 18-year-old's belief in the magic and mystery of the universe. The carriage we were sitting in was on tracks, and as it reached the top, it swung out as if it was going to fly into the sea. I hate the overuse of the word awesome... it was awesome. I screamed out with pleasure and joy. Richard joined me, yelling his own yahoo. It might have been then that I looked at him seriously for the first time. And actually thought, maybe... just maybe... I might let him get to first base.

16

Fate Steps In

During my first three years of college, my life ran on two tracks... stardom and marriage.

At the beginning of my sophomore year, Richard and I began a correspondence that lasted over the next two years. He was stationed at Fort Bragg, North Carolina, home of the 82nd Airborne paratroopers. Whenever he got leave, he would drive non-stop to visit me, making another attempt to "go all the way." Putting off the inevitable, which was only going to happen after marriage, was exhausting.

I went to class like a good little girl, but I scanned the show-business newspapers for auditions. There were always auditions, but I could only go to the ones that fit around my college schedule. I couldn't afford to miss any classes. If the school called my mother, there would be hell to pay. This was the 1950s and I was a student in a public college and beholden to the city's rules and regulations.

Joshua Logan was preparing to direct a new musical called *Wish You Were Here*. He was looking for new talent. A siren call if ever I heard one. The play was written around relationships that took place in a Catskills resort. The big news was that they were going to build a swimming pool on stage for most of the scenes.

This was to be my first professional audition, and it had to be in a bathing suit? Why, God, oh, why did you do this to me? My body was ok in a bathing suit, but my thighs were a disaster. They were too big. They rubbed against each other. I was never going to be mistaken for Betty

Grable but If I sang loud enough and moved well enough, maybe just maybe they wouldn't notice.

My first professional audition was all about my thighs.

If you are planning to audition anytime soon, let me tell you something very important: It is better to go on stage thinking you are brilliant even when you're not – something about having confidence works in favor of the talented or untalented – than to walk on stage filled with self-doubt and fat thighs.

I walked onto that Broadway stage in a darkened theatre with the powers that be seated so far back only a disembodied voice reached me. I was certain the only thing they saw were my thighs. I didn't have a face or a figure. Only thighs that were too close together. I prayed they would look beyond my fat thighs and discover the star that I was and always had been.

I made it through the first round, and then I was cut after the second round. It was clear. They finally noticed my thighs. I rationalized my misfortune: If I had made it into the final round, I would have had to miss class for Broadway rehearsals and performances. My unhappy parents would have prepared some draconian punishment that would make my fat thighs seem unimportant.

As the college years passed, I kept reading the trade papers and trying to find the next audition that would fit into my college schedule while at the same time auditioning for college productions. The drama department at Hunter College was very good. New York City was a mecca for good teachers in the art world. Where else could you get paid and exercise your gift at the same time? Auditioning for college productions was never a challenge for me. My not caring whether I got the part worked in my favor. In the professional world, it would have saved me so much grief if I understood that focusing on what I was doing rather than wondering what they were thinking of me might have made a difference. I never once thought of my fat thighs when I did a college audition.

I worked in one production after the other. In my junior year, I landed the role of Mrs. Webb in Thornton Wilder's *Our Town*. A beautiful play about my favorite subject: death in life.

Richard, though still in the Army, was home on leave. By then, we were definitely "an item." and he came to see my performance. During the first act, I got my period. I was unprepared. Who knows, maybe Richard being in the audience provoked my uptight body. At this point, I had been "teasing" him for two and a half years.

The girl who played Emily had a Tampax. My mother didn't know from Tampax. She knew about sanitary napkins. So, I only knew about sanitary napkins. I had another act to go. My friend stood outside the bathroom door and tried to blindly guide me where to place the Tampax.

Emily: "Sally-Jane, there's only one place the Tampax can go."
Me: "I'm sorry. But I'm finding a few places it can go."
Emily: "That's not possible."
Me: "Oh, my God. I don't have a place where the Tampax can go!"
Emily: "Of course you do."
Me: "I'm telling you I don't. Maybe that's why I hate sex because I don't have all the parts. Oh! It's gone!"
Emily: "What's gone?"
Me: "It must have found its place. How do I get it back?"
Emily: "All you have to do is pull the string, and everything will be fine."
Me: "String? String? What string?"
Emily: "Every Tampax has a string to pull the Tampax out."
Me: "Emily! There is no string. There is no string. The Tampax is inside me, and there is no string. I have a Tampax inside me that doesn't have a string. I'm going to die."
Emily: "Sally-Jane, please calm down. It's there, I promise. Every Tampax has a string."
Me: "Except the one inside of me."

The Stage Manager called 10 minutes until the beginning of Act II. I spent a few more minutes searching every nook and crevice available to my fingers. It would have helped if I understood the female anatomy. As part of my fear of sex, I made it my business to be as ignorant as I possibly could about my body. The string was lost somewhere inside my body. I had to get to the stage. I did the whole second act in a state of mind having nothing to do with Grover's Corners, the imaginary town in *Our Town*. I was waiting for the Tampax to fall out of me onto the spotlit floor and to watch as the audience stampeded out of the theatre in shock and disgust. I imagined being carried out on a gurney, loaded into an ambulance and rushed to the hospital. The Tampax would have to be surgically removed. I would never be able to have children.

The show was finally over. As cast members removed their makeup, I was calling the family doctor, who lived in Brooklyn. In between sobs, I explained where and how I lost a Tampax. I don't remember him laughing. I wouldn't have heard it if he had. I was semi-hysterical. Richard appeared backstage to congratulate me and drive me home to Westchester. Stoically, I informed him we had to go to my doctor in Brooklyn. One look at my face told him not to ask why.

I ordered Richard to wait in the car. I didn't want him to hear my screams. The doctor was very sensitive. I don't think it was a minute after I laid down on his table that he found the lost string. My doctor provided me with a familiar sanitary napkin.

I was too embarrassed to explain to Richard what had really happened. So when I returned to the car, in quivering tones, with a well-placed tear here and there, I told him if he loved me, he wouldn't ask for details. In words, my mother used to explain anything she was too embarrassed to talk about; I informed him I had "female trouble," and the doctor saved me. I would be able to marry and have children. That was all he needed to know.

Of course, I hoped and prayed I would never have to do either because any minute now, I was still going to be discovered.

In the winter of my junior year, I developed a persistent cough. The college nurse sent me for an X-ray. I had a spot on my lung. I was diagnosed with tuberculosis.

Hunter was a public college. I was banned from attending school until my x-rays were clear. That was OK. All I wanted to do was sleep and do my interpretation of *The Lady of the Camellias*. I had a disease. You don't get many acting opportunities like that in your lifetime.

At the beginning of my internment, I played almost dead brilliantly. It was fortunate my sister Lucille had married; I finally had my own bedroom. My dialogue was straight out of a bad movie.

"It's all right. You don't have to worry about me. I'll be gone soon enough."

My brother David, always the jokester, "When?"

Arlene totally ignored me because, finally, my illness took the spotlight away from "the baby."

As I lay in bed and the weeks became months, I began to realize my life, as I knew it, was over. I gave myself over to depression. Depression brought out the very worst in me. I had been diagnosed with tuberculosis and... "IT WAS YOUR FAULT! "

I can't get out of bed. Your fault.
I can't audition. Your fault.
I can never be a star. Your fault.
I can't graduate college. Your fault.
I can't get married. Your fault.

The "your" was anyone who came within earshot of my bed.

I whined and complained about everything. My mother and my brother David ran up and down stairs to bring me hot meals, tissues, medicine, tea with honey, and tea without honey. I hated coffee. I couldn't even play a proper invalid like Elizabeth Barrett Browning. I looked like one of Fagin's beggar kids from Oliver Twist in my hand-me-down red flannel pajamas, lying prostrated under a raggedy plaid beach blanket. I was surrounded by Philistines, my brother, and my mother, who knew nothing about drama or poetry. I had to come up with a plan to prove what a martyr I was to their heartless treatment of me... a gifted, dying artist. I was determined to make them feel as guilty and as terrible as possible. I was going to commit myself to a sanitorium for tuberculosis. That would show them.

As I was about to speak my brilliantly played farewell, the Board of Education notified my parents of an error in the diagnosis. I did not have tuberculosis. I had bronchial pneumonia. Talk about sticking pins into the balloons before the party.

Is it a Plane?
Is It a Train?
No! It's Super Richard!

Beyond everything, Richard was and always would be a brilliant problem-solver because he knew the devil was in the details. He was amazing. My parents, David, and everyone else who ran up and down the stairs during my confinement called him The Rescuer. And he was.

After three months of my whining to Richard on the phone, in tearful resignation, I offered to release him from any "understanding" we had. He was mustering out of the Army. He was in North Carolina. He drove all night.

He walked into my room and told me to stop being a spoiled brat. I was to concentrate on getting better and begin my senior year while he began his first year at Yale Law School. We would become engaged on my birthday in October. We would marry when I graduated so I could get a job and pay our living expenses while he finished law school. We would shop for the engagement ring in a special discount store his mother knew in the Diamond District on 47th Street in Manhattan. What a guy!

I recovered very quickly after that visit. I didn't even have time to regret that I'd have to finish college and wait until we were married to escape my family and become a star, finally. It was obvious that I would have to surrender my virginity before I did another professional audition. I was all right with that. I remembered what Harriet Ferment said, "Every virgin forest needs a man to cut her down."

17

For A Brief Shining Moment

After we married and Richard graduated from law school, we moved to Washington, D.C., for his job with the legal department of a regulatory government agency. Government-speak for another lawyer addition to the already overpopulated bureaucracy of legal beagles. We settled into a wonderful third-floor walkup apartment in a brownstone overlooking Massachusetts Avenue near Dupont Circle, above the offices of an ophthalmologist.

We were at work during the day, so we were never bothered by patients going in and out. The office closed at 5 P.M. Our apartment became a weekend party haven for disparate lawyers and accompanying female clerks and secretaries. With the office closed, we could blast *Rock Around The Clock* to our heart's content. It was like lunchtime at Performing Arts. I still couldn't cook, but I became adept at mixing packaged onion soup mix with sour cream, surrounding it with chips, cutting up a pineapple and sticking umbrellas in the slices, and emptying jars of olives and cans of peanuts into bowls. The lawyers, clerks, and secretaries arrived with either a six-pack or a bottle of vodka. I provided the grapefruit and cranberry juice to make a very potent Sea Breeze. A couple of sips was all it took to release the frustrations of young challengers to the system who were sinking the moment they entered the swamp of government bureaucracies where they worked.

Our families were not subtle about asking for an expected "blessed event." I gave no thought to motherhood, parenthood, or any domestic hood. I had no peripheral vision. Straight ahead to stardom for me. How delusional was that? In the late '50s, Washington D.C. was a cultural vacuum and backwater city.

I told myself I needed to be free in the unlikely event of an audition. I signed on with Kelly Girls, a temporary jobs agency. They insisted on a typing test. I insisted on failing it. I lost count of how many times. I could definitely type the required speed of 60 words a minute, sometimes faster, but what I typed had no relevance to English. I really never got any better, but someone must have taken pity on me, or they had run out of qualified typists. I made my way around the city for a day or two here, a day or two there, getting fired from more than one organization because of my unique typing skills.

I scoured the papers for auditions that didn't exist because theatres didn't exist. Finally, I spotted an advertisement. Maybe it wasn't an advertisement. Maybe it was just an announcement in the society pages of *The Washington Post* that the Hexagon Club was going to produce its annual charity revue and was looking for talent. *Looking for talent? Hallelujah!*

I had no idea, nor did I care what the Hexagon Club was... a witch's curse? Here was the audition I had been waiting for. I entered a church community room with my 8x10 glossy, my resume, and music. After singing, reading a sketch, and making some dance moves with the other auditioners, I realized why no one came professionally prepared: because they were not professionals. I was the fox among the chickens. These amateurs did a musical revue once a year as a benefit for a chosen charity. I was starving... thirsty... staggering in a desert of cultural want and need. I hid my credentials.

The best part of the Hexagon experience was the young reporters for major newspapers and news services and budding diplomats who did most of the writing. This was 1957. Eisenhower and his crew came in for some first-rate political ribbing. A society charity revue was the only place you could get away with ridiculing the President and his administration. Except for me, the female cast members were all society Blue Book Debutantes. Thank goodness I was a great pretender. It wasn't easy. A Jewish girl from Brooklyn didn't have a lot in common with Bitsy, Betsy, and Bootsy.

I converted my New York accent to the debutante drawl; "I caun't tell you how graund to...".

While I was performing at Yale, I used my whole name on a program: Sally-Jane Heit-Schwartz. The student in charge of printing said I needed to make a choice – too many names wouldn't fit on the program. So, with Richard's permission, when I performed I was Sally-Jane Heit. What a guy!

Introduced as Sally-Jane Heit, it took a while for the debutantes to connect my husband's name – Schwartz – to mine. Not too many Schwartz, Cohens, Goldbergs in the Blue Book. It wasn't overtly anti-Semitic. It doesn't have to be, does it?

The show was a fantastic success, and so was I. I starred in a couple of Hexagon shows over the next two years.

Enter the 1960 Presidential Election.

The Kennedy campaign brought with it a youthful exuberance and humor not seen before in a statue-infested, Southern conservative, overly formal, and formulated Washington, D.C. This was an administration that had fun and made fun of themselves. The climate in Washington, which had previously been hot and stuffy, became cool and open. Kind of! Hexagon writers and other writers who had been hiding in the woodwork of the Washington scene were emboldened to experiment with an old form of political satire, the cabaret theatre. Included in this political send-up time were international groups like *That Was The Week That Was*, *Beyond The Fringe*, and solo cabaret performers like Mort Sahl and Mark Russell.

Some writers I knew convinced the owner of a very fancy French restaurant in Georgetown to open his second-floor private party room as an experimental political cabaret. It really was a no-brainer. We were center stage of every political issue, scandal, personality, and government agency. When Watergate was happening Mark Russell said he took a vacation from writing. He'd go to the ticker tape and tear off enough for a show and, standing up, read it off the tape or put it to music. Atop this elegant Georgetown restaurant, The Uniquecorn was born. A quartet of two funny guys, one short, one tall, and one normal female, and one brash, big-mouth blonde that critics called "Washington's own Carol Channing." Though I hated the comparison, it was good for business.

By this time, Richard had insinuated himself as the business manager into our little troup. He was show business addicted. We performed nightly. Professional actors and directors, musicians and writers seemed to come out of the woodwork because, at long last, there was a place to ply their talent. The woodwork was the agencies of the United States Government, which employed most of them. Euphemistically, they had "day jobs" waiting, like me, to be discovered. Talent isn't the only ingredient for discovery. You need luck, which includes being in the right place at the right time. Washington, D.C. was not the right place for theatrical and performing talent, but our unique little troup was an oasis of creative work for displaced "artists."

During the run of the Uniquecorn, I made some lasting friendships. My best friend was a gifted housewife named Shirley. She wrote the most sublime satirical music and lyrics. She was older than I was, so her window of opportunity to follow her passion was non-existent. She had a husband and four children, and she lived in the suburbs. She wrote shows for her Synagogue. She had a cache of songs she wrote just for herself. I knew from the moment I heard her songs that I had found my artistic doppelganger.

Our funny/sad conversations were filled with children/ husband problems, and a very mutual yearning to be discovered.

Shirley: "How did it go tonight?"
Me: "They loved *Starve a Fever, Feed a Complex Waltz*."
Shirley: "Oh, that old thing."
Me: "I had an idea."

Shirley: "I'm afraid."

Me: "What if we wrote a show about two housewives and how they struggle to write a show about being more than a housewife?"

Shirley: "Meshugana, babydoll, and ultimately boring!

Me: "Why?"

Shirley: "Did you enjoy reading about yourself in *Diary of a Mad Housewife?*"

Me: "I resent that. I am not crazy."

Shirley: "Yes, you are. How about a new song about your first period?"

Me: "Now, who's crazy."

And we both were.

Lord, thou artest everywhere, artest'nt thou?
I know thou hast beenest here Want to knowest how?
Thou gave me my period on the 5th of July
And I never even toldeth the nurse or the counselor, either
Lord, thou really scaredest me
Lord, was it gross
I thought tonsils were the pits
Tonsils were the toast
Lord, I'm glad that's over
Cause I never have to have it again
AAAAmen!

Oh, Lord, I really miss this woman.

There were some exciting moments in our cabaret theatre life. The owner of the restaurant was well-satisfied with the publicity and the profits.

Visits from the Kennedy administration personnel sent a flutter through everyone's celebrity thermometer. No sightings of the brothers, JFK and Bobby. I actually received an invitation to perform at LBJ's Vice Presidential mansion in honor of his daughter Lynda's birthday. And no, I did not sing "Hello, Lyndon" to the tune of *Hello Dolly*. But they were gracious, and I received a Steuben glass bowl engraved with directions to the LBJ ranch in Texas. Ah, if only I could translate glass lines.

Washington, during the summer months, is unforgivingly hot and swampy. Before air conditioning, diplomats from foreign countries assigned to the nation's capital received hazard pay. The cast and our music director voted to take the summer off. Not me. I asked the restaurant owner if I could use the room each Thursday to Saturday to put on my own show. He had a soft spot for his "Carol Channing" star and agreed.

I asked Shirley to play piano for me. My idea of two housewives doing a show was not so stupid after all. The incongruity of it all was pretty damn funny. Shirley looked like a housewife. Hair barely put together. No makeup. Not even lipstick. And a figure that had never seen the inside of a gym or knew from a pair of shorts or sneakers. Her dress was something she would have worn to Synagogue on Saturday morning. What the audience saw when she sat at the piano was a middle-aged woman who most likely gave piano lessons to the neighborhood kids. What they didn't see was the very fine musician who had studied long and hard before marriage and who could write music and lyrics that were smart, outrageous, and oh, so very funny. I was the glitzy contrast. Well-coiffed, made-up, and brightly costumed with sparkles and sequins. I looked like I belonged. Shirley did not.

We were a hit.

18

And Then There Were 3,4,5...

Richard decided it was time to silence our families' persistent, "So.... any news???"

Deferring to Richard was as natural to me as figuring out another way to avoid sex with him. Nine months later, in the last month of 1959, my beautiful miracle daughter was born.

I would like to omit the story of her birth. My ignorance on so many levels is shocking. My first labor pains began December 7th or 8th. I am not quite sure because I didn't know if what I was feeling was labor or gas. The spasms were few and far between. The stories I'd heard from women who experienced labor were all about excruciating, never-ending pain. For me, it was a shot of pain. Wait a few minutes. Another shot of pain. It could be gas. I called the doctor. He suggested we wait. We waited.

As long as I was at home, it was easy for me to label what was happening as gas pains because I had experienced them before. I didn't understand the basics of my anatomy. I had this huge contoured bowl extending out from my body. A baby was inside this bowl. That baby was two weeks overdue and needed to come out. I knew nothing about how that was supposed to happen. My ignorance was purposeful. What I didn't know wouldn't hurt me. I had a vague idea of how the baby made its way out from my body but damned if I knew what body parts were involved and how they were connected.

When the contractions had begun, I did my best to imagine it wasn't happening. The next day, when the contractions, though still far apart, were consistent, my imagination stopped working. Richard couldn't wait to drive me to the hospital. We called the doctor again, and he told us to go to the hospital. It was December 8.

Virginia Woolf published her famous essay, *A Room of One's Own*, in 1929. Expectant fathers of the '50s already had a room of their own... the waiting room, not for Richard. He went to the office. The doctor said he'd call when the contractions increased.

I was taken to the labor suite. I didn't see Richard again until ten hours later when I insisted he take me home. During those hours my Doctor had delivered two other normal babies of normal women with normal labors.

After listening to the moans and screams from the surrounding suites, I asked if there was such a thing as a scream-proof room.

Nurse: "What a sense of humor. You're funny."

It wasn't funny. If my baby didn't want to come out. That was fine with me. But I was done. Maybe there was no baby. Maybe there never was a baby. Maybe it was all just gas. I didn't want to stay there.

Finally, the doctor decided, for the safety of the other mothers, it was best to let me go home. Richard picked me up from the hospital. It was December 9th. We went home. I was upset with Richard. In every movie I saw, the father waited in the waiting room. Richard had failed me.

A few hours later, a rhythmic pattern of contractions began. The doctor said to return; back into the labor suite. By this time, I had been in labor on and off for about 36 hours. Alright, already, that's enough!

Early in the morning of December 10th, my first daughter, Dianne, named for my mother Anna and the Goddess of the Hunt and the Moon, middle name Rachel, for my mother's mother, was born. Information to be discarded: my uterus was heart-shaped, and therefore, the ability to have steady labor contractions - impossible. Here, for me, is the $64 million question. Knowing that this was likely to happen again, what form of insanity is it that makes any woman return to the scene of this happening?

I don't know what it is for anyone else but I think there is a mechanism within the mind-body connection that dims the memory for these return engagements. The simple answer is that we women have a lock on the miracle of birth. If you are into having children, which I didn't know I was until I had the first one, experiencing that miracle is pretty damn brilliant and intoxicating. As a practical matter, every time I went into labor, Richard could always count on extra hours at the office.

From the moment of that first birth, nothing was ever the same for me. It may seem unseemly, but it's like death; no matter how prepared you think you are, you are not.

Richard showed up for the births of all three girls. It was almost as if he was the local parish priest, giving his benediction then leaving to get back to Church, aka his office. Seven days a week, 12 hours a day for the next 15 years, that took its toll on everything and everyone.

After her birth, Dianne survived only because of my mother's insightful gift of hiring a nurse for the first two weeks. When this woman arrived, almost immediately I saw the resemblance between her and Mother Theresa and Mary Poppins. She was going to save me and my baby. The poor woman. I couldn't leave her alone.

Knocking loudly on the bathroom door, "Hurry up. Please. I just checked Dianne. She stopped crying. Her eyes are closed. We have to call the doctor."

Drying her hands as she opens the door, "I just rocked her to sleep. Do not call the doctor."

Obviously, I was not natural mother material.

Dianne was so teeny tiny. I was never going to be able to pick her up and feed or change her. I was never going to be able to wash her. She would always be dirty. She was too damn fragile and small. Whenever I watched the nurse do anything, it was like watching a come-alive

73

documentary. I remembered watching one about male penguins being the caretaker for the baby penguin. Oh, to have a live-in male penguin.

At the end of the two weeks that I had my Mother Teresa/Mary Poppins, I got down on my hands and knees and, like a penitent, prostrated myself before her, begging her not to leave me alone with my daughter. I don't think the nurse ever looked back. She must have been so happy to be able to go home to her own bathroom.

How in hell did I fold a diaper for this teeny tiny body? They were cloth, large, and inflexible. What was the secret formula to putting this huge diaper on this ridiculously tiny body? And please, God, tell me why she never stopped crying. Dianne was a baby with colic. She cried all the time. Later, it became apparent why, but before I knew it, when she cried, it was clearly something I did or didn't do or should have done that made her so unhappy. Well, of course, it was my fault. After the nurse left, there was no one there to argue or disagree with that fact. I had one consolation. There was data somewhere that proved a colicky baby was the cause for the commitment of a certain percentage of first-time mothers. I was not alone.

Lori arrived 18 months later and joined the routine of a live-in baby nurse followed by a less terrified second-time-around mother who was more knowledgeable, not necessarily comfortable, about the routine of rocking crying babies, feedings, diaper changing, and cleaner babies. This nurse was allowed proper bathroom breaks.

Eighteen months after Lori was born, our last-ditch effort for a boy baby (I can't believe I allowed myself to be part of that kind of patriarchy), Pamela arrived on the scene.

My only relief came with whatever show I was doing at the time. It was my performing that kept me from being committed. However, it also made me a poster woman for the perfect bad mother. No other woman I knew put her children to bed and then left them for a few hours every evening. Except... right... streetwalkers. We had a common bond. We performed out of need and deed.

19

A Married Single Mother

It was my overpowering sense of guilt, which somehow blended with my overpowering need for love, that saved us all.

By the force of their needs over mine, the arrival of Dianne, Lori, and Pamela pulled me away from myself enough times in life and brought me into a new world, their world.

Against my will, my priorities changed. There was no way I could ignore their cries for food and other basics. Oh, believe me, there were many times I wanted to. Every time I thought about sneaking out to a movie, I knew I would not be able to hear what the actors were saying because my earballs would be filled with the cries of my hungry babies. Lonely and exhausted and pulled in all directions every other minute, against my own judgments and prejudices, I began to need them as much as they needed me. That need increased over time.

Dianne's "best friend" in elementary school turned traitor. Elizabeth switched her allegiance to the "in" crowd for an invitation to a birthday party Dianne wasn't invited to.

"Di, we're going to have a party."
"It's not my birthday."
"It will be in six months. We'll have a before-your-birthdays birthday party, and we won't invite Elizabeth."
"I want to invite Elizabeth."

How do I support and defend Dianne if she won't let me send out a contract on Elizabeth?

Non-competitive Lori became Richard's target for criticism and judgment.

Richard: "Why can't you be more like your sisters?"

Where had I heard that song before?

Lori: "I don't like to act. I hate basketball."

How do I support and defend Lori if I can't send out a contract on Richard?

From her earliest years, Pamela always had words. She could defend herself against any of my or Richard's words and thoughts. No subject was taboo from her querying mind.

"Mom! How old were you when you first had sex?"
"Pammy, let's wait till you graduate kindergarten... or until you begin menstruating."
"That's where you're wrong, Mom. We should talk about this before I get my period."

She was right, of course. So I took her to the obstetrician who delivered her and said, "You tell her."

It wasn't just that I was a coward, but I was still a little dumbfounded and confused by body part placements and functions.

The girls filled the vacuum that Richard had left. When I was with my girls, I was less lonely. Oh, not to worry, I was still the loud, brassy blonde who wanted to be a star, but maybe not at all costs. I began to understand that babies just need love and protection until they can protect themselves. The damn cloth diaper is the only change required.

The girls grew up surrounded by a variety of motley, temporary live-in helpers and babysitters of every stripe and color. Some better than others. To my shame, it took a while before I fired a Bible-thumping punisher. Catching the end of her sermon to the girls about how they were born in sin was her last day. I had a couple of gay guy sitters that were fantastic. Dianne, Lori, and Pamela had an advanced education while in their care... often R-rated. These guys were fun and they treated the girls like people, a fact often forgotten. I had old costumes hanging in a closet. They did their own drag shows before any of their friends knew what a drag show was.

The countdown began after dinner. After bathtime, I went from bed to bed to sing *Over The Rainbow* and a beautiful lullaby written by Shirley as I petted and kissed my girls goodnight.

A Giant, A Giant, your old mommy is
No, I'm little too, little one.
So you fit in my hands, well I fit in HIS
So I'm little too, little one
The sky and sea they look to me
Like your room looks to you
So don't be afraid
The hand at your cradle
Is so little, too, little one

If the sitter arrived by the time I finished the song, I tiptoed out of their room and ran like the devil to make the half-hour before the show call.

If the babysitter had not arrived by the time I finished the song, I bagged a bunch of pillows, wrapped my girls in warm blankets, put them in the car, drove to the theatre, put on my makeup and costume as I settled them on the pillows on the floor of my dressing room; Dianne sneaking out to gossip and giggle with the cast, Lori with her art pad and colored pencils, and Pammy with her book. She was the only one to really sleep until the last curtain call.

Once my sister Marilyn and her husband Sam and their six children moved into a suburb of Maryland, I never had to use my dressing room as a nursery again. She opened her house, her heart, and her wonderful family to my girls.

I adored my girls and loved them all to pieces, but the movie had already been written... *Fabulous housewife, mother, and soon-to-be star discovered hidden in the Rotunda of the Capitol.*

When the children were out of school, during the summers, I would take them with me to various summer stock theatres. One summer, at a theatre in New Hampshire, the director, after having met the girls, assumed I had been married three times. He couldn't believe they all came from the same mother and father. They were so very different from each other.

They were loved. Probably not the way they wanted to be. But then... who is?

20

Local Diva

With three young children, I was very bizzie... driving to piano, dance, sports, arranging child care, promoting and performing, doing minimal wifely duties (sex), and becoming a big fish in the small pond of theatre in Washington, D.C.

During the course of my summer show with Shirley, I gathered a group of FWM (fans with money) that made it an easy step from the cabaret atop the restaurant to a full theatrical production of my first one-woman spectacular.

"Miss Amurica" opened at The Washington Theatre Club in November 1963. The reviews were disastrous. After years of being the fun, funny girl of D.C. (Isn't *that* an oxymoron?), it seems I had lost more than my sense of humor. Of course, the reasons it failed are aglow in hindsight.

The whole enterprise was pathetic. I was out of my depths. I had a captain who had never been on a ship, and as first mate, rather than focusing on the material and performance, I surrendered to my ego and to personalities that were going to "do" something for me. Shame on me. The show was doomed even before we opened.

The only good thing about the whole experience is that I knew the show didn't work. Being able to critique your work is a basic element of an artist's gift.

A week after I opened, President John F. Kennedy was assassinated. The world stopped. The show closed.

Richard and I took a bus downtown. We had spent hours getting into the Rotunda to see Kennedy lying in state. Thousands of people, shocked and muted, shuffled towards the Capitol like shackled lifers, our emotions numbed by the hours of having watched the tragedy unfold on television day after day after day and now standing in line for a last look at a fallen hero. A constant bitter reminder of what a heartbreaking loss the country had just suffered. We walked to Constitution Avenue to stand for hours with thousands of others as we silently watched the tragic funeral cortege as it made its way to Arlington National Cemetery.

Life changed.

I could not make sense of the world or of my failure. Worst of all, I bought into a deep depression experienced at one time or another by most of my fellow artists. I was a fraud. I was delusional. I had no talent.

Richard was a problem solver, not an empathizer. Emotions, his or anyone else's, were beyond him. He had no solutions for a failed show. I was left alone to lick my artistic wounds and for the first of many times to come, I contemplated giving up the theatre.

Along with millions of other Americans, I limped out of 1963.

I swore to spend more time with my children and fake more orgasms. The latter being more difficult because Richard was always at the office.

21

My Rude Awakenings

I t was the '60s, and homophobia was rampant. Over the years, as Richard slaved away nightly at the office, I acted as a date, aka beard, for my many gay male friends. I was grateful. I was never at a loss for an escort to the theatre or concerts. It's difficult to imagine today how threatening life was for a gay man. All professions were infected by fear of discovery.

One evening after the theatre, one of my "dates" dropped me at Richard's office.

I walked in on a scene from a bad movie. Richard and Betty, his attractive administrative assistant, were going at it on a desk.

They froze. I froze.

Like a robot, I backed slowly out of the door I had just entered, closed the door, waited enough minutes for clothes to be rearranged, and knocked very loudly on the door.

Whatever time I gave to both of them, I gave to myself so I could erase from my mind what I saw. It had never happened. Like the great actress I knew myself to be, I played the scene. When Richard opened the door, I leaned in to give him a quick cheek peck. His very tall, very redheaded, very bosomy assistant was putting away papers and packing her briefcase. I chatted nervously about the show I had just seen. I had absolutely no memory of that show. No problem. I made it all up. I rattled on about my "date" dropping me off so he wouldn't have to drive me home.

Richard was relieved. Phew! I was not going to make a scene. Betty just stood at her desk, reshuffling papers from here to there and back again.

"That's fine. We were just finishing up. Just give me a few more minutes, and I'll be happy to take us home."

That was my *Ripley Believe It Or Not* moment. I actually convinced myself that I did not see what I saw. My brain couldn't handle it. In any language, it's called denial. I'm not the first and certainly not the last to deny a truth if I felt it threatened my life.

I was 31 years old, and my life was over. My behavior towards Richard changed completely. He was never to be trusted. And I never did.

Our tenth anniversary was coming up. I did not want to celebrate with Richard. I might have denied what happened, but these new feelings about Richard had to be expressed somehow. He had played the role of the '50s husband and father. It was 1963. Relationships and roles were beginning to change. Other friends who were fathers babysat their children, changed a diaper, came home for dinner. I didn't understand why I was so angry and resentful. I just was.

The anniversary symbol for ten years is tin. What is it the Tin Man in *The Wizard of Oz* asks for? A heart! I needed one badly.

Between my failed show and a failing marriage, the world that I thought I created - happy wife, happy mother, happy performer - disappeared.

God was having another big laugh. I was a woman responsible for three attention-starved children. There were days I couldn't get out of bed, do the laundry, or make lunch. For dinner, opening a can of Spaghettios was asking too much. Ploddingly, I put one foot in front of the other to get through each day. With two toddlers and an infant still in diapers, that was all I could manage.

Like a bad Joan Crawford movie (think Mildred Pierce), I announced I was going to celebrate our anniversary alone and visit my mother.

"OK. I'll take care of the girls."
"I think not. I shall be taking them with me."

He didn't put up much of a fight.

22

Help Wanted

I was so relieved when Mother gave me permission to visit. I needed to ask her a very important question. My father had passed away years before. She lived alone in the house that I left when I married Richard. There were four bedrooms and two bathrooms. All those rooms for one person.

I arrived at my mother's house on my tenth wedding anniversary. Of course, she was immediately suspicious. She was always suspicious. She had brilliant antennae. I fed the children and put them to bed. I sat in the kitchen to talk to my mother as she prepared our dinner. I stuttered through the explaining of the disaster of my marriage. Of course, I couldn't use the most damning evidence – his infidelity – I had buried that.

Damn! Haltingly, I logically recited my reasons for wanting a divorce. However, as I continued, my pent-up emotions exploded into hysterical ranting. I was crying, twisting my rings, and my nervous knees were shaking a mile a minute.

"I have three children. He never sees them. He's never home. I am alone. I'm a single mother. He refuses to babysit. I can only perform if I can pay for child care. I have to get another job to help pay for our house bills."

I took a deep breath and finally came out with it:

"Mom, you have a big house. I can move in with you. Audition for shows in New York. Become the *Star* you always wanted me to be! Remember when I was Aunt Lily's little Shirley Temple? I don't have any money, but I could clean the house, do the shopping. I would get a part-time job to contribute to the bills."

Sobbing incoherently, "You were right. You are always right. Marriage is nothing but sacrifice and suffering. I am so very alone and unhappy. Can I divorce Richard and move in with you?"

During this pitiful monologue, my mother never stopped what she was doing. She never once looked at me. And when I was finished, she said,

"Do you want your lamb chops medium or well done?"

The silence of the lamb chops was deafening.

I can only guess at the level of my desperation. What was wrong with me? How could I even think my mother would hear my plea, no less respond to it? My mother was almost seventy, and after raising eight children, she was tired. It was now clear. I had nowhere to go. No divorce.

The next morning, I repacked the girls into the car and drove away from her house, minus a plan to escape my marriage.

I was at a crossroads. At the invitation to stay at a friend's house, I was going to Martha's Vineyard for a week of beach walking and contemplation.
I think it was somewhere close to the Connecticut state border, on the Merritt Parkway, when a pain coursed through my gut so intense, so frightening, I almost lost control of the car. I finally maneuvered it off the highway and onto the grass. My breath came in short, extremely painful bursts. The pain was so intense it forced my head to the wheel. The girls sat frozen in terror as I dropped my head and moaned.

I knew I was dying. There was nothing I could do. The pain was unrelenting. I had no sense of time, but as I was breathing my last, someone knocked on the driver's window. With great difficulty, I lifted my head off the wheel. It was a State Trooper.

"Everything all right, ma'am?"

What a question! Am I alright? No, officer, I am not alright. I just died. But thanks for asking.

No response from me.

"Is everything alright, Ma'am?" he repeated

The pain began to subside. I began to breathe normally.

"Yes, Officer. I am so sorry. I just needed to pull over and close my eyes for a minute."

I'm sure he thought, *Yeah, right! This woman must have been on some bender last night. And with three kids in the car. I ought to arrest her.*

I didn't care what he thought. I had no idea what had happened. All I knew was I wasn't going to die. My children were safe. Traumatized but safe. I thanked him for checking on me. And drove off to the Island, having just experienced my first panic/colitis attack.

I spent the week walking the beach, making sand castles with the girls, watching sand crabs appear and disappear. Oh, to be a sand crab.

Nature is always transformative for me. Martha's Vineyard in June 1964, was very quiet. Through the limitless horizons, dazzling sunrises and sunsets, shifting tides, and endless waves I was constantly reminded of just what a tiny spec of flotsam on the jetsam I am. If I could breathe, I could heal. If I could heal, I could think. The rain and biting cold wind pierced my thoughts and offered me what I needed most: solace and perspective. I was one with the natural Universe. Off the Island, the damn human one gave me grief.

No rescue. No escape. For better or for worse. Oi Vey. Dianne, Lori, and Pamela were stuck with a committed and responsible mother. At least on certain days of the week. Double Oi Vey.

Richard loved his girls, no doubt. But we all knew what his priority in life was because, without the girls, it would have been mine.

But I had birthed these miracles and however ignorant I was, and believe me, I had no idea just how ignorant I really was. I loved them and I was going to see them through high school and headed towards their choices in life before I left.

There was no money for a divorce. I became the kind of wife Richard needed: First, you see her, then you don't.

When the time was right, and I was sure I would know when that was, I would find a new rescuer, preferably in New York City, and exit... stage left.

Oh, yes, my friends, old dreams die hard. It took me years to realize that love that asks for any payment was not only expensive and luxury but not love at all.

I returned to D.C. with a revised plan for myself.

If I were an accountant, I would advise the decade of the '60s to file for bankruptcy.

1963!
1964!
A failed show!
Adultery!
The assassination of John F. Kennedy...

It was never going to be repeated. Right??? Wrong!!!

1965... Malcolm X
1968... Martin Luther King and Robert F. Kennedy.

All right, already, STOP!

Animals only kill for survival. What does that say about the human condition?

23

Open Marriage

It Never Entered My Mind
Lyrics by Lorenz Hart Music by Richard Rodgers

Once, I laughed when I heard you saying
That I'd be playing solitaire,
Uneasy in my easy chair,
It never entered my mind

And once you told me I was mistaken,
That I'd awaken with the sun,
And order orange juice for one,
It never entered my mind
You had what I lack myself

Now, I even have to scratch my back myself.
Once, you warned me that if you scorned me
I'd say the maiden's prayer again,
And wish that you were there again,
To get into my hair again

It never entered my mind
It never entered my mind

The '70s brought in the Moral Majority against the background of the immoral and amoral Vietnam War. This was a perfect backdrop for the publication of the best-selling book *Open Marriage* by George O'Neill and Nena O'Neill.

Richard was too busy to read books. He read this one. He asked me to read it. He wanted me to be interested in what the O'Neills believed: A sexually non-monogamous marriage, aka an open marriage, was good for the husband and the wife. Having sex with another partner outside the marriage made it stronger and better. No wonder it was a best-seller. No wonder he wanted me to read it.

What I knew about sex would be lonely in a thimble. In the 1950s, as a girl raised by Victorian parents, I had two choices. I was either a saint or a slut. My emotional and physical experience around sex was traumatizing. The seed of fear planted very early was fed by the sexual revolution of the '60s and the open marriage book of the '70s. And now, I was being encouraged by my husband to leave the convent.

I can't say exactly when I went from being shocked at the proposition to accepting the proposition. Timing is everything.

In the 1970s, I no longer lived with my parents, but I was still a 1950s girl. There were many more categories of females beyond saints or sinners. When being a virgin lost its market value, both men and women were open to different arrangements. I had several close female friends who were already living the double life with a lover and a husband. They were only too happy to share their soup and sex recipes. This Alice, aka Sally-Jane, was becoming curiouser and curiouser. I convinced myself I was the only one holding me back from a new life.

Like most important events in my life, I backed into my open marriage. It helped that I was very angry with Richard. It was his fault I was alone most of the time. It was his fault I was mother and father to the girls. It was his fault I had to pay for the babysitter. I wanted to show him that without me, he would be busted and broken. By the time I finished plotting the movie that would prove this truth, I knew Lana Turner, Better Davis, and Joan Crawford would kill each other to star in it.

I opened up an economy-sized bottle of aspirin. I flushed all the tablets down the toilet. I left the empty bottle and cap on the sink for Richard to find when he arrived home. Surely, when he saw it, in profound shame and grief, he would realize what he had done. He would save me and promise to babysit any time I wanted and ask for sex only once a week.

Prior to his arriving home that night, I positioned myself seductively on our double bed wearing his favorite nightgown, hair brushed and flatteringly arranged on the pillow, a little color on the lips, and blush on the cheeks. I was irresistible.

I heard him come in around midnight. I feigned sleep. He tiptoed into the bathroom. I heard the empty bottle hit the empty garbage can. That was it.

I was done. My headball went immediately to what was good for the gander was going to have to be better, much, much better for this goose.

Of course, my first attempt at an affair had to be with someone I knew. A family friend. No strangers for me. Before marriage, I was a professional tease. I made anyone I ruffled my feathers at think they were going to score. Even after I was married, I never really stopped flirting. Flirting resulted in attention. Attention resulted in performance. Performance resulted in appreciation. And the leg bone connected to the ankle bone. Taking it from flirting to the actual affair took some profound denial and rationalizations. It was performance art before there was performance art. My performance took place in a hotel room instead of a theatre.

Fred was part of our group of lawyer friends, and I knew he had a large sexual appetite. His wife told me. She warned me to be careful of him. He warned me to be careful of him. We were all very careful. I met him in a three-star hotel room in New York, accompanied by the occasional cockroach. I arranged the assignation while I was visiting my parents. I knew Fred was interested in me. Every woman knows when a guy is interested. Physically, I may have avoided it, but intellectually, sex is a basic animal instinct. He had put out feelers before, and I had always rejected them. He was as surprised as I was when I responded positively the next time he showed interest.

Of course, the experience terrified and excited me. As the sordid scene unfolded, I felt as if I were watching it from across the room. What Fred was doing paled in significance as I worried more about the state of my underwear. Did I wear the bra that had a safety pin that held up the torn strap? Were my panties the pair with the stretched elastic?

I remember clearly what I was doing: nothing. First, I stood still and let him have his way with me. Then I lay still on the bed and let him have his way with me. I was so embarrassed. What kind of an idiot chooses a full slip instead of a half slip? All that extra action just to get through the top of the slip, then the bra to feel real skin... mortifying.

My greatest acting came after. Trying to be casual and sophisticated, smoking the cliché after-sex cigarette while waiting to be struck by lightning from the vengeful, righteous Sunday School know-it-all-God who was permanently affixed inside my brainball, I was very worried. Even after giving birth to three babies, I still didn't quite know where everything was. No one ever claimed having sex or birthing babies made you smart, and I was stupendously dumb. I imagined Richard would know the next time we had sex.

Sally-Jane! I know someone has been here before me. Who the hell was it?

Yeah, I actually thought somewhere in my private parts, there was a mechanism that would tell the present occupier that there was someone in there before him.

I did it a few times with Fred before we realized renting hotel rooms was an expense neither of us could explain or afford. The sex never really got any better, but it was fun to have a secret that made life a little more exciting and interesting and appeared not to hurt anyone. What can I say? I was young and stupid.

When I met a new male friend, Dennis, from a summer stock engagement, he didn't realize that as we rehearsed, he was also auditioning as my next partner in open marriage. It was good to be good-looking, but it was more important that he be funny. If I think about it, laughing took some of the onus away from what I was doing. If

I laughed at what I was doing while I was doing it, it couldn't be so bad, right?

Two or three of my plus-ones became dear friends who took the time to tutor me in the art of sex and explain which parts of my body did what. Unconsciously, because I was married with children, I chose men who didn't want commitment. The market was full of them. In my business, sex was what to do at night after the show or when the theatre was dark.

All the while, a soundtrack began niggling its way inside my brainball. Not quite Peggy Lee's *Is That All There Is*, but closer to, *There's Gotta Be Something Better Than This* from *Sweet Charity*. What was wrong with this picture? Why weren't Richard and I enough for each other? It takes a hell of a lot of energy and planning to have affairs. Not only was it dissipating my relationship with Richard, but I began to realize my energy and focus – always in a battle between children and career – were being further debilitated by these affairs de corps.

I began asking myself, "Why am I doing something I really don't want to do?"

The denouement of open marriage occurred at the closing night party of a summer stock production of *Hello Dolly* in North Carolina. I had been having a good time with a fellow actor whose wife was not happy about her husband playing around with me. She drove from her home in Virginia to the theatre in North Carolina and crashed the party. She had done her due diligence and knew who my husband was. I had no idea what she looked like, so I was unaware of her marching over to Richard to confront him. I missed the whole damned scene. Richard reported it to me in bravado detail. She had asked him if he knew that his wife was having an affair with her husband. Richard was born for this moment.

He looked at her Clark Gable-style and said, "Yes, I did. And I don't give a damn."

She was gobsmacked.

Throughout the five years of my open marriage experience, Richard and I never openly admitted having our affairs. We knew. And we declined discussion or prosecution.

I was a stupid woman who actually believed I could have the love I needed from partners other than my husband without any consequences. In truth, I was getting away with absolutely nothing.

In the years of my open marriage, no one had ever accused me of anything. What I was doing had been recommended in a book millions of people read and followed. I deluded myself into thinking our marriage was better for it. Someone was always around to give me the "love" and attention I craved while Richard was at the office. I omitted from my thinking the fact that while at the office, he was receiving his own satisfactions. No one was being hurt.

I couldn't have been more mistaken. After digesting what Richard told me about this woman's accusation at the cast party, I was mortified, embarrassed, ashamed, and more sorry than I had ever been in my life for anything I had ever done before. What I was doing did hurt someone. I wasn't able to understand how much I hurt myself until years later.

I think what finally broke through from my subconsciousness was Richard's gesture of forgiveness. Like the High Priest of his own religion, making an improvised sign of the Star of David, he forgave my infidelity.

Double, double toil and trouble,
fire burn, and cauldron bubble
SHAZAM!

My anger mushroomed like an erupting volcano. The memory of that night when I had walked into Richard's office and found him and his female assistant in flagrante delicto rose from out of my subconscious in cinemascopic technicolor. In that moment of hypocritical forgiveness, the falsity of our so-called open marriage exploded. I was totally aware of the role I played in this farce of a marriage. I had lost the right to point a finger at anyone. And I didn't.

I knew I was done with this hypocrisy and his wandering eye. Done with my complicity in accepting that as acceptable and done with looking for love from someone else.

For me, the open marriage of our marriage was closed.

24

Coat of Many Colors

E very summer, we had an opening of the pool and deck party. One of my neighbors, Mary, was a psychotherapist. I called to invite her. Before she hung up, a voice from out of nowhere asked if I could come to see her professionally.

In the world of privilege, therapy opens the door to self-examination. There is no possibility of change without that very painful process. It didn't take long for me to realize that I had found a safe place to open up about my life. Of course, I started with the movie version of my life. Mary waited me out until I was ready to give her the real story. The one without flattering lights, a backup chorus, or clever script. She never once challenged me. She did what no one in my life up to this point had ever done. She listened. She had no answers. Listening is so powerful. It gave me the strength to slowly and safely unravel what I felt were the criminal parts of my life. And even then... no judgments, no criticisms. I was thinking of making things up just to get a rise out of her. She was not shockable... all the fakery, the lies, the pretense, the affairs.

Her questions brought me to the beginning of each lie, to each affair. A blind man could see the pattern of my behavior and where it came from. She led me through the valley of the shadow of my life without needing to blame anyone, least of all myself. She gave me the courage to face me without makeup. In a certain light, I didn't look that bad. If I wanted... only if I wanted... I could change what I thought was unchangeable. Oh, it weren't easy. One step forward. Two steps back. The days I am open to examination of my behavior are the good ones.

I wanted to share the value of therapeutic help with my daughters. I wanted them to have a safe space to express themselves. I searched for and found a great child psychologist, Edna. Once a week over their Junior High School years, they went to see her, sometimes one at a time, sometimes together. She opened a path to an invaluable tool for growing up: establishing boundaries. Boundaries? What the hell was that? Borders of a foreign country, right? Dianne, Lori, and Pamela didn't need a passport to have a conversation with their mother, did they?

I was devastated. Every boundary established moved them further away from me. I had a husband in name only and lovers who left on a schedule. I was emotionally dependent on my daughters being emotionally dependent on me. They were the ballast that kept my ship afloat.

Dianne: "Mom, Edna says having a mother as a best friend is not a good thing."
Lori: "I love you so much, but please try to understand; I have a guidance counselor now who is helping me choose my program."
Pamela: "I'm going to spend the summer with Catherine and her family. I knew you wouldn't mind."

I had created therapy monsters. Despite my controlling and neediness, they were growing up. If I didn't want to lose touch, I had better catch up and grow up, too.

Thank goodness I had my career. I was the Queen of Dinner Theatre in the D.C. area. I starred in every major musical: *Guys and Dolls, Damn Yankees, Gypsy, Anything Goes, Once Upon A Mattress, Fiddler On The Roof...* If it was on Broadway and it went to dinner theatres in suburban Virginia and Maryland, I starred in it.

As I performed in all these shows, I thought I was doing really good work... until my friend, Nick, appeared in a pre-Broadway tryout at the National Theatre. I did not allow myself or him to know how envious I was of his opening in a show on Broadway.

On his day off, I invited him to see me play Mama Rose in *Gypsy* at the dinner theatre. Due to its popularity, the show kept being extended. I was sure I was giving Ethel Merman a run for her money.

After the show, we settled in my living room with a drink and a cigarette. Yeah, those were the days.

He said, "Sally-Jane. You are good. Too good to be dessert."
"What???"
"You can act and sing your heart out. But in dinner theatre, the play is not the thing. The drink and the dessert are."

Stupefied!!!

"All your years of study and working don't mean anything if the eyes, ears, and minds of your audience are eating or drinking or waiting to eat and drink."
"But I get standing ovations every night."

Nick gave me the look that needed no dialogue.

"Mama Rose is a great comic/tragic Shakespearean character. Don't sell her or yourself short."

I acted as if I would seriously think about what he said. I even thanked him for his critique. I drove him to his hotel.

All the way home, I wailed and bitched and thought about finding a hitman. At the same time, I knew Nick spoke the truth. I also knew he took a huge gamble in telling me this truth. My most common human failing is the ability to deceive myself. In my need to perform, to be loved and secure, it wasn't the first time, and it wouldn't be the last time I took the road most traveled.

25

At Liberty

I f I wasn't going to do dinner theatre, where was I supposed to work? In the '70s, Arena Stage was the only game in town. The major productions of Ford Theatre, the National and Schubert theatres only produced road company shows. No Kennedy Center yet. Along with those limitations, I wasn't an easy actor to categorize. The label that followed me most of my career was, "You're special." This had a variety of meanings. Too big, too blonde, too too... "Thank you, but no thank you."

I bless the director of a small equity theatre struggling to stay alive in D.C. (not for long), who cast me as a Chinese mother who owned a laundry in Murray Schisgel's comedy *The Chinese and Dr. Fish*. With a black wig, constantly differentially bowing, hands together, and only speaking Chinese (phonetically), I got a laugh before I opened my mouth.

At the very beginning of his career, somewhere in the 1940s, Tennessee Williams wrote a one-act play, *At Liberty*, about an out-of-work actress. In the theatre, "at liberty" is a nice way to say *"no job."* I couldn't have been more than 15 when I played that actress at Performing Arts. The thought of not having an acting job frightened me.

For most actors, "out of work" is synonymous with being out of sync in your life. If I can't act, I can't breathe. It's the lucky ones who have creative and fulfilling hobbies... painting, potting, knitting, tatting.

I was not one of the lucky ones. I had two left hands. I was dispirited and depressed. And then...

William, a reporter in the entertainment section of *The Washington Post*, had been kind and generous in his reviews of my work. We had met socially, and I praised his writing and critical talents. Alright, already, a little self-serving but also true. It would have led to a conflict of interest if he hadn't decided to leave *The Post* and travel to Paris to study at the Cordon Bleu. He had always wanted to cook and write. We kept in touch.

Upon his return to Washington, D.C., in the late 1970s, he took a job with a start-up wine magazine, creating wine-pairing menus. When the first issue was published, I decided to show my support for his new job by inviting eight people, including him, to dinner. I was going to prepare the menu he had created. I had not really cooked again since my potato salad debacle. For all its use, the kitchen would have made a good closet. Our dinners consisted of foods that were faster than any fast food drive-in could deliver. Monday, hamburgers; Tuesday, hot dogs; Wednesday, spaghetti and meatballs with canned sauce and leftover hamburgers; Thursday, McDonald's; Friday, pizza. On the weekend, I stretched my culinary gifts, baking chicken wings covered in Kraft Catalina Salad Dressing.

My friend William admonished me, "If you can read, you can cook." Well, I was a big reader... easy-peasy.

The core of William's special dinner, taken from his magazine menu, was a Butterflied Crown Leg of Lamb. Sounds pretty. The piece de resistance dessert? Baked Alaska.

I found a local butcher and ordered the lamb. When I picked it up, the ribs had all those cute little paper frills on them. How sweet.

I was confused by the one difficult ingredient in the recipe – clarified butter. I didn't understand what that was. After much cogitation, I came to the conclusion that it was a kind of grammatical description of butter. Since I was looking at butter, this clearly was a past participle kind of butter, i.e., clarified. Sounds good to me.

I had a little difficulty with the little paper frills on the crown roast. I ran out of them because they all burned in the first hour of cooking. You are supposed to put them on after you roast the lamb. If it wasn't written in the recipe, it wasn't going to happen. I substituted little cocktail umbrellas to decorate the lamb. They looked really cute. This time, I waited until the meat was done, or overdone, before decorating it.

The guests arrived. Everything that could go wrong did. Thank goodness I knew the secret ingredient for any impending disaster... wine! If you pour enough wine, no matter what's in front of you, the dinner works.

My timing was completely off. When cooking, you have to plan what dish is prepared first. Each part of the menu has its specific timing. There was no script to memorize. I was out of my league. I was forced to serve the brussel sprouts as the appetizer. I thought they were done. They weren't. They were inedible. Pour the wine. The lamb was overcooked. Pour the wine. I had to change the garbage bag several times.

At least the umbrellas were a hit. With nothing to eat, we played Snap the Umbrella. Pour the wine. The umbrella roast was unaccompanied by any side dishes because I had either served them before the roast was ready or I was waiting until they were finished. Before going into the kitchen to check on dessert, I poured everyone a large glass of wine. I opened the oven door. The baked Alaska had melted all over the oven shelf. Thank goodness I kept drinking the wine along with my guests. I would not have had the courage to make an announcement,

"The baked Alaska melted onto the bottom of the oven. I can offer spoons if you're into scraping up what you can. Furthermore, I forgot the tea and coffee, but there's one more bottle of wine."

And then, like the Queen in *Once Upon A Mattress*, which immodestly I played brilliantly,

"You are divine. Get out."

Of course, I was mortified, embarrassed, and ashamed, and I begged William's forgiveness. I had to wait until he stopped laughing before he told me I deserved a medal for attempting to climb Mt. Everest in toe shoes. He was enthusiastically overwhelmed by my audacious support. That day, in the kitchen, with the debris of the disastrous dinner all around us, he promised to make me his sous chef and teach me how to cook. And he did.

Fast forward to his new job as Food Editor for *The Washington Post.*

We had already cooked some meals together. William's friends, my friends. He equipped my kitchen with proper knives. You can't cook without a good knife. Together, we made excursions to the store to expand my seasoning repertoire beyond salt and pepper. Slowly, I realized I had found my "at liberty" hobby. Cooking, as I discovered, satisfied my creative juices. I could sing, dance, make funny faces, and, for the first time, make an excellent potato salad.

William's success grew, as well. He wanted to invite master chefs who visited Washington, D.C., for whatever purpose – honors, book signings, testifying –to dinner. It would be the perfect way to create menus for his weekly food section while providing an opportunity to explore different cuisines with top chefs. The only problem was that William was a bachelor with a one-bedroom apartment with a small kitchen and virtually no entertaining space. I had a big old-fashioned house with a big old-fashioned dining room and kitchen to match. The *Washington Post* would pay for the food and wine, and I would volunteer my talents as the kitchen slave, along with the use of my house.

I knew nothing about celebrity chefdom. I lived in a world of children and show business… culinary stars were far removed from my orbit. If I wasn't watching an episode of *I Love Lucy* with my kids, I was auditioning for my next job.

William announced he was going to cook for his good friend from Le Cordon Bleu, who was visiting D.C. on a promotional tour. I checked my calendar and said it was a go. We invited the usual suspects to make it an even twelve around the table.

Prior to Julia and Paul Child's arrival, William informed me about Julia's fame. I had no idea. Julia was plain-spoken and charming, and I liked her immediately and immensely. Paul was a bit more of a puzzle. The table was filled by a great group of people with Julia at the head.

Do not expect me to remember the menu. It was at the beginning of my apprenticeship, and I was buried in details that had nothing to do with the menu and everything to do with getting the parsley more finely chopped. I do remember the first course was soup. William was in the kitchen putting the final touches on each bowl before I brought the soup around. I served Julia first and went back into the kitchen for the next bowl. When I returned, Julia was slurping away.

"Hey, Julia. Hold it. I have eleven more bowls to serve."
"Sally-Jane! (in that fantastically wonderful inimitable voice) Did you work hard preparing this soup?"
"Julia! Are you kidding? We've been chopping and clopping and schlepping and cooking for two weeks. Damn right, we worked hard."
"Is this soup supposed to be eaten hot?"
"Of course it is."
"Well then, I am going to eat it as it is supposed to be eaten... hot!"

What a woman!

Every time William and I held a dinner, I would put my daughters to bed with their lullaby and my version of *Over The Rainbow*. They always managed to sneak out of their beds and sit at the top of the stairs to listen to the old folks talk, laugh, eat, and drink. That night, they overheard Julia.

Henceforth and forever, on being served, I was certain to hear three chirping voices in chorus,

"Mom, I'm not waiting. This is supposed to be eaten hot."

There were no state secrets. But this was Washington, D.C., and between the worlds of journalism, culinary arts, and show business, we managed to have some interesting conversations with some interesting people. Richard adored the dinners. Mr. Questionmark (his middle name) was always a good conversationalist. Most of the guests loved being interviewed. Also, he didn't have to do anything. As ever, he was a guest in his own home.

I shall always be grateful to William for introducing me to cooking as an art form. Being "at liberty" in the kitchen was just fine with me.

26

Back To What I Do Know...

O pening myself to more theatrical opportunities became all-consuming. It was easier to find those opportunities during the summer. Washington, D.C., in summer, was a hazardous swamp filled with politics and the weather. For those who could afford it, wives, mothers, and children escaped to the beaches and the mountains for two months, leaving a howling pack of male summer widowers. We couldn't have afforded that particular privilege. Still, Richard was one of those howlers. That was just fine with me. For ten glorious years, I would pack the car with three children, taking all their paraphernalia, a babysitter, and the family dog, and head to East Carolina State University in Greenville, North Carolina, where I spent ten glorious years in summer stock, performing in all the brilliant '50s, '60s, '70s musicals in a 1,800-seat theatre with a 26-piece orchestra and Broadway-quality sets and costumes and direction and choreography. And this time, I was not dessert.

My experience culminated in a wonderful production of *Hello Dolly*. In truth, I would have much preferred to play Dolly Levi in Thornton Wilder's *The Matchmaker*, from which *Hello Dolly* sprung. Such a brilliant play. A role made memorable and incandescent by Ruth Gordon. Still, it wasn't bad to be in what was Gower Champion's brilliant achievement. He created and choreographed the best manufactured standing ovation moment in theatrical history.

On opening night of *Hello Dolly*, as I made my parade around the outer rim above the orchestra dressed in white with a white feathered hat that weighed a ton while the cast serenaded me with the pulsating, pounding rhythm and lyrics of *Hello Dolly*, 1,800 people stood up and applauded my circuit through the whole song and the many encores that followed. A moment of triumph for any actor.

Later, at the opening night party, I received flowers and accolades, and somewhere in the middle of the raucous noise, I slipped away into a room with a telephone. I called Richard. I was sobbing. He thought the show had failed. I told him it was the biggest success the theatre ever had. A sold-out run of two weeks. What was the problem, he wondered?

I sobbed, "The whole audience of 1,800 people gave me a standing ovation."
"I'm confused. Why aren't you ecstatic?"
"They weren't standing up for me. They were standing for Gower Champion."

Whoever wore that white dress and the hat that weighed a ton and walked a circuit as the cast and orchestra beat out the tune would get that audience up on their feet whether they could act or sing or not. Of course, it was better if you could sing and act, and if you had a pinch of charisma, better still. No matter. This was a classic manufactured moment for audience and lead. It had very little to do with Thornton Wilder's play. Oh, the show had the characters and the plot line, but the heart of the play and the depth of the characters were missing.

Years later, Bette Midler made my point. On certain nights, for whatever reasons, she ignored the book of the musical *Dolly* and improvised and traded jokes with the audience. No denying the audience loved her. Talk about standing ovations. I'm not so sure Thornton Wilder would have stood, not to mention the cast members who were dependent on her giving them their cues to re-enter the show as written.

But, back to my opening night. *Hello Dolly*, opening night.

Richard did not understand what or why I was blabbering. I barely understood. I was experiencing what I call a "Peggy Lee moment." In her sexy, smoky rendition of *Is That All There Is?*, she asked the question I would philosophically, artistically, emotionally, forever keep asking myself... *Is that all there is?* A standing ovation without personal artistic merit was just another way of being dessert.

I was becoming a critical curmudgeon. Nothing was satisfying. No husband. No love affair. No hit show. No domestic satisfaction.

No matter how I tried to hold back the dawn, my daughters grew. As firstborn, Dianne suffered the longest from the slings and arrows of an ignorant, outrageous mother and father. Some of her scars were visible. She had a quick temper. She was smart and sassy, and in junior and senior high school, it appeared she was headed for a career in the biz. Dianne sang. She danced. She acted. She was good. I was proud. It all came to an abrupt end in her first year of college. A college, by the way, that had a respected theatre department. Dianne never went near it. At the end of her freshman year, I asked why.

"I am not going into competition with my mother."

To prove she meant what she said when she graduated college, she left for a study program in China. Could you get any further away from your mother?

To this day, Lori is more empathetic than most humans I know. I swear she has a genetic condition that senses and feels for others. She always thought of others before she thought of herself. Maybe it's part of middle-child syndrome. Of all my daughters, she was sensitive to my loneliness and frustration. It was bad enough being born between two overachievers, but she had a mother who unconsciously took advantage of her empathy. I had a close friend who left the theatre to become a psycho-drama therapist. I shared with her my feelings about taking advantage of Lori.

She suggested we role-play.
I didn't have to audition. So, why not?

At first, I played me, and my friend played Lori. Even though she didn't know Lori, there are benchmarks for children of a certain age, so she was believable. Then we switched, and I played Lori. Out of my mouth came such pain about not being seen or understood. She (I) cried about not wanting to have to be like her (my) sisters. She (I) just wanted to be herself (myself).

I couldn't believe it. I was me, and I was Lori. I knew exactly what Lori was going through. Our entire relationship changed. I gave up having answers. Well, almost. I tried to allow her to map and plan her life. Ultimately, she chose to listen to herself not me.

By the time Pamela was born, I understood she carried within herself all the necessaries for her development. I gave her a wide berth to be who she was. She was someone with a gifted tongue. She communicated her needs without any hidden agenda. She was more authentically herself than many at her age. If she had an issue with me, I never had to wonder what it was. It wasn't that she didn't love me. She did. She just wanted a different mother. She wanted the stay-at-home mothers her friends had. On some level, I wanted to be that mother for her. On another level, not only did I not want to be that mother, but I didn't like that stay-at-home mom. Whether she intended to or not, that kind of mother-of-the-year, on every committee, champion baker of bake sales, always there with a smile and an invitation to dinner when I was late from rehearsals, made me feel more guilty. Pammy didn't want a star. She wanted a mother.

All of my children have always had a yin-yang relationship with my performing career. They loved what I did. They loved to come to my shows and watch me perform. They could sing all the songs. Mimic the dances and dialogue. Pretty funny to see my three young girls doing their version of the stripper's song from *Gypsy*.

They loved sitting in the theatre when the audience applauded and laughed. A golden moment when their pride in my talent came together with their love.

They hated the rivalry between my passion for the theatre and home. Dianne, Lori, and Pamela had a mother who sounded an awful lot like Popeye, "I yam what I yam." It was always going to be a contest. And it was a contest I could not and did not win. As long as I worked at home during the school year and took them with me to summer stock, I was able to fool myself.

As the girls got older and pursued their individual interests, all separate and varied, organizing and scheduling became a nightmare. I didn't mind because the insanity of ferrying each of them to their various dance, arts and crafts, and sports activities gave me reward points. Oh, what fools we mortals be.

27

One Door Closes, Another Opens

I wasn't prepared for my mother's death. No one is. There's always unfinished business.

"Okay, Mom, no one is listening. Now you can tell the truth. You always loved me best."

She was gone. I regressed into a forty-one-year-old thumbsucker. Without the body representing the holy grail of affirmation, what reason did I have to be alive?

There were many months of disbelief, sadness, and within me, a vacuum, an emptiness, a god-damned big hole. I knew what was finally going to happen. The vast emptiness inside of me caused by my mother's death was going to expand, and finally, I would disappear.

Before I disappeared, I went to the movies. Every day for months, I got up out of bed, made breakfast for the girls, shooed them off to school, went back to bed for a nap, then finally rose from my bed, dressed, and headed for the double feature. I went in with my breakfast and lunch and came out in time to pick up the girls for their after-school activities.

The pincher... the hair puller... the judge... the jury... gone. She was gone.

Everyone was sympathetic but shock and pity don't last forever. Life has a way of having its way. I don't remember if it was during a bathroom break between features or a week when I just couldn't see the same damn movies again; a thunderous thought struck me. I had to say it, think it, be it until it finally registered in my brainball. She was gone. If I wanted to, I could go to New York and she would never know. I had opened that can of spinach, swallowed it down in one gulp, and, like Popeye, shouted to the world, "I yam what I yam."

The girls were in Junior and Senior High School. Every Monday through Wednesday, I traveled to New York in search of my elusive star. I would return on Thursday to replenish the larder, the laundry, and the love. Not from Richard. We were reduced to ships passing in the night. I wanted, no, I needed love from my girls. Teenage daughters, protecting their damn boundaries mixed with resentment for my choices, made any expression of love as ridiculous as expecting me to give up the theatre.

Friends from my previous life in New York and New Haven and summer stock had apartments in the city. At different times, they would be off on tour, and in exchange for watering plants, collecting mail, and feeding cats, I had a free bed. I slept all over the city. *By myself.* I was too busy pounding pavements, dragging my bedraggled body and three large plastic shopping bags from one location to another: one for my clothes and makeup, one for my music and props, and one for my resumes and 8x10 glossies.

The only agent who would sign me was Marvin, a college classmate who gave up acting for agenting. He thought I was a star in college. He still believed I could be a star. That and a token would get me on the subway. I auditioned everywhere for everything. Nada!

I did manage to perform... for free. If a cabaret had a platform and a piano, I claimed it with my music and my props. I did a lot with scarves and an old telephone receiver. New York City had a bountiful harvest of good pianists.

Cabaret owners hardly auditioned acts. And even if they did, they never really watched. At no cost to them, it was a win-win situation. We performers filled their spaces with friends and relatives who bought their inedible food and watery drinks. Occasionally, by accident, an agent, casting director, or producer wandered in. It was a rush to see which act on the bill that night would ambush him or her first. No one sent a card back that read, *You were wonderful. Come see me in the morning about a contract.* Only in the movies. Oh, please, if you have the time, see Dustin Hoffman and Warren Beatty audition for an agent in one of these cabarets in the cult movie *Ishtar*. Priceless.

Every week, I would take the bus or the train up to the city, towing my three plastic shopping bags. Over the weekend, the guilty hausfrau in me took over. Monday, Tuesday, and Wednesday, Lori, empathizer extraordinaire, would remove my prepared food from the freezer and put it in the oven. With that incredible second sense she had for others, Lori supported me by becoming the mother in my absence. She had a hard time getting her sisters to listen to her. They had an easy time taking their anger at me out on her.

In the city, I could get any cabaret I was willing to pay for, but for all my efforts, I couldn't get arrested by casting agents, producers, theatre companies, etc.

I was old. In my forties. In all their Broadway show movies about being discovered, Mickey Rooney and Judy Garland, even when they were older, were portrayed as teenagers. When I was a teenager, I loved looking older. No producer-director, Broadway or Hollywood, wants an actress who looks her age. They were casting 40-year-olds with twenty-year-olds... younger is easier on the eyes and the box office.

No one had ever heard of me. My training was good, but what had I done since 1954? It was the '70s. In theatre speak Washington, D.C., was the place they sent movie and theatre stars to testify, to ruin their lives and careers, or to unsuccessfully beg for support for the arts.

I found an extraordinary human and talented New York-based musical director, Robert Bendorff. He was a brilliant composer and lyricist whose sense of humor and absurdity was the glove for my hand. Even with his gift, though, I didn't make a dent in the Broadway firmament.

Year after year, moving from pad to pad, feeding kitties, and watering plants, I was getting nowhere fast. It wasn't fair to Lori. The girls were growing more and more resentful and angry.

Richard's growing success made him even less accessible to me and the girls. What the hell was I doing? If I ever asked that question, it'd be over.

I asked.

From the last borrowed bed, I packed my three shopping bags to begin my exit from Broadway. All ready to go, my failed actor college-mate agent called to tell me that Michael Bennett of *A Chorus Line* fame was beginning a new workshop. *A Chorus Line* also began as a workshop. This was to be a new musical adapted from a wonderful television show, *Queen of the Stardust Ballroom*. Marvin said there was a part in it for me.

My first reaction was, "too late." I was going home to be a big fish in a small pond. Marvin wasn't taking no for an answer. He had a "feeling." Damn! He was the only one who had ever sent me out to audition. What the hell! What's one more time between friends?

Backstage at the audition, I asked the stage manager to watch my three plastic shopping bags. I took my music out of one and my resume and 8x10 glossy out of the other and walked on stage at the Shubert Theatre.

It was a magical time for me. It wasn't just my body that was on that stage. All my dreams came with me. I was lifted away from everything that came before me. I wasn't nervous. I was home.

I gave my music to the accompanist. I chose *It Never Entered My Mind* by Rodgers and Hart as my farewell to New York song. What can I tell you? It was the song that kept me company in my loneliest nights in Washington, and it was my New York state of mind.

I didn't sing to those watching in the darkened theatre. I sang to and for me. I finished. I turned to walk off stage. Michael Bennett, the man himself, strode down the aisle to the stage.

He wanted to know, "Where are you from?"
"Washington, D.C."

Looking at my resume, he said, "You went to school in the city, but you have no New York professional credits. Why?"
"I lived and worked in Washington, D.C., with my husband and three daughters."
"Thank you."
"Thank you."

He went back to his seat.

I picked up my three plastic shopping bags and treated myself to a taxi to Pennsylvania Station. Took my scheduled train home.

I was sad. I was also a little happy. I knew what it felt like to perform on Broadway, and I had met one of my theatrical heroes, Michael Bennett.

28

The Storm Moves To Broadway

O ver the next three months, I was summoned back to New York six times to audition for the featured role of Helen, the sister-in-law to the lead, Bea. After the first re-audition, I was excited but cool. I knew I was up against some of the biggest names on Broadway and in the movies. I told myself the only reason they were auditioning me was because they were filling their quota of available middle-aged actresses. I did not stand a chance. By the time I got to the third audition, despite my trying not to hope, I hoped. Before the last two auditions, I kept myself steady by convincing myself there wasn't a fat chance in hell I would get that part. By the time the number four audition came around, I began to think I just might stand a chance. This is really dangerous thinking. This is the time they bring in the ringer. Like a dear friend who was all but guaranteed the "meat-head" son-in-law part in *All In The Family*, and at the last minute, they gave it to Rob Reiner.

When Marvin called to tell me Michael Bennett was offering the role of Helen to me, I wanted to ask him if Angela Lansbury had turned it down. I didn't. I went through every color of emotional disbelief. Everything was based on fear. I had fooled them. I was a fraud. They were going to discover I had no talent. Those thoughts found a comfortable home inside my headball and kept popping up at the most inauspicious times throughout my whole performing life. Slowly, in exhaustion, I began to accept that I had been chosen. Michael Bennett chose me.

It occurred to me that only *after* my mother passed away, I won a featured role in a new Broadway musical. I think I need my therapist.

The incredible machinations and manipulations that were going to happen because I had a family, a husband, a house in one city, and a job in another city would be dealt with when the time came. Off, way, way way off, a new star gave off a tiny twinkle.

I discovered that one of the reasons it took so many auditions was because of my age. With no New York credits on my resume, the casting director actually called my agent to get assurances that I had not been tucked away in some sanatorium or institution between the years I went to school in New York and returned.

There were two six-week workshops. Michael Bennett followed the same rules he had applied to *A Chorus Line:* Each actor and dancer received a one-dollar recompense for their work during the workshops. In return for our work, the cast and the company received a share of stock in the show. If the show was a success, like the original actors in *A Chorus Line*, we could make millions. Everyone gladly signed on to *Ballroom*.

The workshops were a financial burden for me because I commuted between New York and D.C. I needed to find an apartment where I didn't have to pay rent. Isn't that an oxymoron? My three plastic shopping bags were already packed. If the police would have allowed it, I would have been happy with a bench in Central Park. I did not care! I was going to Broadway.

A favorite relative of mine who traveled a lot had just moved into some pretty fancy digs in the city and saved the day when she agreed to let me and my three shopping bags camp out in the spare room. Without her help, I never would have been able to take the job.

I shall never forget the day of the first reading of the already retitled *Ballroom*, formerly *Queen of the Stardust Ballroom*. Seated in a circle on stage at the Public Theatre in Lafayette Square, New York City, were the major stars of my profession, collaborating to bring this show to Broadway. I could barely contain myself. Titans of Broadway during the '50s, '60s, '70s, '80s: Robin Wagner, sets; Theoni Aldridge, costumes; Tharon Musser, lighting; Joseph Papp, co-producer; Alan and Marilyn Bergman, lyrics; Billy Goldenberg, composer; Jonathan Tunick, orchestrations; Michael Bennett, director/choreographer. Shut my mouth!!!

The cast was introduced. I didn't recognize anyone except the woman, Dolores Gray, who was playing Bea. She was brilliant opposite Gregory Peck and Lauren Bacall in the comedy movie *Designing Women*. When my name was mentioned, a shiver went down my spine. OMG, how did I look? Where was a mirror when you really needed one? I just kept smiling. I stopped only to say a line. I tried desperately not to watch to see what the reactions were to my readings. *Keep cool, baby. Pretend like this isn't your first time around the block.*

"My goodness, I've lost count of how many pre-Broadway table readings I've done."

Too cool. Not believable.

When I got a laugh... oh, praise be to heaven... the actor's credo, *they like me.*

Seated outside of the actor's circle were the dancers. Former gypsies, aka chorus boys and girls from every major and minor musical of the '40s, '50s, '60s, are now cast as middle-aged ballroom dancers for the show. For me, forever, they were the stars of *Ballroom*. I watched every night from the wings as they did their foxtrot, waltz, lindy hop, rhumba, samba, and salsa numbers. The show should have run forever so the world could see that age is really a state of mind. All right already, at least until they got some money back for working for nothing for those workshop months.

After the reading was finished, I was dumbfounded. They had what I believed was the most important ingredient in a successful show: a good play. It's not a myth. The play's the thing... direct from the man who should know, Shakespeare. Why were we doing a workshop? *Ballroom* was already there. Let's just go into rehearsal and get this show on the road. That's how much this old/newbie didn't know.

The talented artists sitting around this table were eminently human. Like all of us, their egos and insecurities accompanied them wherever they went. The director's most important job was to corral and unify the collaborators' egos and insecurities towards a singular vision of the play.

Notes from Professor Heit's Production 101 lecture: Following Aristotle's theories of unity, the director's vision inspires his or her collaborators to exercise their gifts towards this one vision. You need a sober, strong, conscious visionary to humor, encourage, challenge, and occasionally berate these various artists into bringing their disparate gifts into this unified vision. *Without this unified collaboration, a Broadway failure loomed.*

Our leader, talented as he was, riding on the waves of his first blowout all-time winner, had a few problems that would doom *Ballroom*. Fame did a number on Michael Bennett's head. And like many theatre people, Michael was superstitious. Never put your hat on the bed. Never say Macbeth while in the theatre. Worst of all, he convinced himself that no matter what he did for his next project, the critics would not let him have another success immediately after *Chorus Line*.

The cast kept changing throughout the workshops, keeping my paranoia active and healthy.

Since dance was Michael's gift, he worked mostly with the dancers and the choreography. He hired joke doctors to rework and rewrite the play.

By the time we made it to Stratford, Connecticut, for our pre-Broadway tryout, the script had changed from a heartbreaking story of a lonely widow and unhappily married mailman meeting in a ballroom to a joke-filled non-dimensional sad story of a lonely widow and unhappily married mailman meeting in a ballroom. It all came to a head for me at a rehearsal in Stratford only a few weeks before our Broadway opening. I had just been handed a new script for a scene between Dorothy Loudon and me, the new Bea. The lonely widow Bea wanted the family to understand she was happy. Helen, her judgmental sister-in-law, though critical of Bea, had always been thoughtful about her. In the new pages

I was given, whatever humanity Helen had was removed and replaced by one joke after another joke. I knew Michael had just hired a new script doctor. There had been many before this one, but this one was famously funny.

If Michael kept to what he knew – *A Chorus Line, Dream Girls* – he couldn't miss. Glitzy show-businessy stories. But *Ballroom* was about plain, ordinary people living plain, ordinary lives. The story was completely outside our esteemed director's experience and understanding.

After reading the new scene I was so disappointed. I walked onto the stage at the Stratford Theatre. Our leader, the new funnyman writer, and all the other powers were sitting in the back of the theatre. I didn't think about what I was doing. I couldn't have stopped myself if I wanted to. Shouting out to the back of the house, minus Joan of Arc's armor and sword:

"Michael, I just read the new scene. My character is funny because she is the judge and jury of this family. Nevertheless, in all previous scripts, she was at least human... very real. (waving the paper). In this, she has no humanity or dimension. It's just line after line of jokes."

That is the essence of what came out of my mouth. Maybe not so succinctly. Definitely not so succinctly. I'm betting there was a lot of "uh," "you know," "um," and "well." The passageway between my brain and my mouth was on overload. It didn't matter. For a "what's her name," I had crossed an uncrossable line. There was a pause that definitely did not refresh. I was Jonah. The whale had just opened his mouth. And would you look at that? All by myself, I walked right in.

Eventually, from the back of the theatre, Michael spoke, never getting up from his seat, "Sally-Jane!"

Oh, my goodness, he remembered my name.

"Do you want to open on Broadway in two weeks?"

That was a stupid question. Of course, I did.

"Do the new pages as written."

The silence that followed was deafening. No discussion. No consensus. No exchange of ideas.

If you don't have the power, the clout, or the money, then neither the answer nor the question matters. Never challenge a dictatorship. That day on the stage in Stratford, I discovered that producing a show is a power-driven autocracy. So what else is new? I coulda, woulda, shoulda said, "If it means denuding my character and thereby weakening the core of the play, NO! I quit!"

I didn't.

There are some compromises that don't hurt. This hurt. I knew they were eliminating the soul of the show, and it wasn't for the better. And I also knew that, in some small measure, I had sold off a piece of my own soul to open on Broadway.

We opened on Broadway. After which Michael, the last of the big time spenders, rented out the brilliant Windows On The World restaurant atop the World Trade Center. Richard and the girls, looking for celebrities, were in attendance. I stood in the corner by myself, crying. Just like I had after I opened *Hello Dolly* in North Carolina.

I knew.

Richard asked me why I was crying. I told him that in order to run this big-budget musical, we needed what is euphemistically called a money review. A review that was so brilliant that people would stand in line for tickets for years. A *My Fair Lady,* we were not. The reviews weren't horrible. The critics listed all the pluses, the choreography, the middle-aged dancers, the actors. Yes, I even got a shout-out, but the big minus was the play itself.

I was in serious trouble. After being away from the farm for so long, the idea of returning home was unthinkable. What the hell was I going to do?

Thank goodness my good friend Charles, a professional stage manager, had the chutzpah to put it to me. Throughout the workshop, rehearsals, and the four-month Broadway run, I whined and complained about how the book of the show was being destroyed.

In irritation, he yelled at me, "If you don't like what you're appearing in, write your own damn show."
"I'm not a writer."
"Then shut up."

I couldn't write. But I had friends who wrote. I could sing. Maybe I could put something together. Right? Of course, right! I needed a new show as much as I needed my next breath.

29

The Gathering Storm

*B*allroom closed in March of 1977. I had half of an old one-woman show put together. I returned to Washington. I needed help from my D.C. team of writers, most particularly Shirley, whose songs were the backbone of my shows. Between myself, Shirley, a few writer friends, and a lot of old material, I would put something together. I was clear. I needed a vehicle to get me out of Washington and back to the Great White Way. The material was immaterial. The producer/director of the theatre in North Carolina, Edgar, where I performed ten years of summer stock, offered a smaller theatre on campus for the tryout. He generously promoted the new/old show *Dolly Returns as Sally*.

After the failure of *Miss Amurica* in 1963, I couldn't believe I was putting myself in harm's way again. Doing a turn in a cabaret is vastly different from playing in a theatre. In a cabaret, if the audience doesn't like what they're seeing... have a sip, take a bite, talk to your mate, all accepted behavior. Not so in a theatre. Without distractions, I had to capture their attention and keep them with me as long as I was on that stage. I must have had a memory lapse or, at the very least, early Alzheimer's to return to the theatre. It was a calculated risk I was willing to take. If I did a one-woman show, I would have a modicum of control. If I waited for some producer/director to cast me in a new play, I had absolutely no control. I needed to get back to Broadway NOW.

Dianne was in college. Lori graduated high school and chose to travel. Pammy was a senior in high school; one foot was already out of the door. Richard returned to his previous act of pretending he wasn't having sex with his secretary. Living in D.C. without my daughters was not an option. I had a lot of material. Some good, some not so good. Most of it showed the wear and tear of time. No matter. The sheriff and the posse were after me. I needed to get out of town... fast.

As I gathered material, a few months before I left D.C. for North Carolina, Lily Tomlin brought her Broadway one-woman show, *Appearing Nightly*, to the National Theatre.

The only Lily Tomlin I knew was the *Laugh-In* comedian. She was funny. But a whole evening in the theatre of one person who didn't sing or dance... couldn't possibly work. Cullen, a summer stock friend, had a day job as Lily Tomlin's driver and offered me tickets to her show. Life was never the same.

In wonderment, I sat in my seat while the theatre emptied. Then Cullen asked if I'd like to meet the star. What a question. Does a bear do "it" in the woods?

We went backstage. Appropriately, I kissed Lily Tomlin's rings. She was kind. She was generous. When I finally got my tongue to work and my vocal cords to emit sounds, I told her the show was stupefyingly brilliant. Jane Wagner, her partner in life and also the writer of the script in which Lily Tomlin played to perfection the various people and situations the two women had encountered over their lifetimes, was in the dressing room as well.

Stupefyingly brilliant!!

That damn voice again. You know, the one that I didn't recognize as mine blurted out that I wanted to do what Ms. Tomlin and Jane Wagner had done. I explained that in a couple of months, I would be performing a one-woman show in a small theatre in North Carolina. The material was a pastiche of old and new material written by others. Now that I had seen Lily Tomlin's show *Appearing Nightly*, I knew that would be a terrible mistake. I wanted to begin from the beginning and create the situations and the characters that revolved around my life experience.

Ms. Tomlin must have caught the sincerity, dare I say the desperation, in my voice. Right then, in her dressing room, she sat me down. She, Jane, my friend Cullen, and me. She explained how she and Jane slowly... oh, so slowly... put this show together. They had traveled from one coffee shop, cabaret, church basement, and performing garage to another, writing one sketch at a time, followed by performing each sketch. Throwing out what didn't work. Rewriting what almost did.

On the one hand, it was obviously a long, hard slog. On the other hand, the slog satisfied. *Laugh-In* fame brought investors and theatre owners to secure a Broadway run.

The characters Lily and Jane developed came from a more diverse universe than mine. More sophisticated, political, and worldly. Mine was the world of sit-coms: husbands, wives, mothers, children, suburban sex. I stole and exaggerated characteristics from my life as a guilt-ridden, duplicitous, wannabe, control freak perfectionist. It was a laugh a minute.

Lily Tomlin's story was like a torch to the dry kindling that had been inside my headball for years. Over the next ten years, between the girls developing in every sense of that word and a husband who was never there (which got to be a good thing), I wrote. I created some pretty interesting characters. My favorite was one of Harriet Ferment's best friends, Edith.

Edith couldn't tell you how many men she bedded during her marriage because she stopped counting after twenty, or was it thirty? She spoke brilliant psychobabble from all her years of therapy. Eventually becoming a therapist, and in her society-debutante drawl, babbled advice to her latest conquest.

Tony, Tony, Tony...(pause) Tony, Tony, Tony...(pause) Tony! You will notice, Tony, I am not angry. What is anger? A manifestation of guilt. I have no guilt. Consequently, I have no anger. When I manipulated you into the actuation of this relationship, I was aware of where you were coming from. I was able to get behind that. And bearing in mind that our relationship was, to a certain extent, ego-satisfying and occasionally sexually significant. I knew we were coming from two different places. We are light years of levels apart from each other. Light years of level, level, levels apart.

I challenged myself to create characters that made me laugh and cry. Marsha, the closet lesbian who sounded like a truck driver and never got over her fetish for her father. Dork Grossman, the lawyer Lothario, who settled parking tickets in exchange for a roll in the hay. Carmen, Harriet's pretty size-five sister, who ran away with every man, including Harriet's husband, Franklyn Ferment. Tomlin and Wagner's show opened my mind and soul to the absurdities of the human condition... especially mine.

30

The Perfect Storm

I had an inner elevator that was out of service. It was permanently stuck in my subconscious. When I created Harriet Ferment, I was in total denial that she resembled me in any way. I thought of myself as the all-together, put-together, successful, funny lady who managed everyone and everything to perfection. It took a lot of denial not to see the elephant in the room.

Harriet was a housewife, mother, and lawyer whose life was perfect, perfect, perfect. She had the best parents, the best husband, the best daughter, and the best career. She gave the best advice, the best parties, the best sex, and climatically, she had the best breakdown. Like Nero, who played a bad violin while Rome burned, Harriet was both sides of the comedy/tragedy mask, but for the most part, she was absurd.

I wrote Harriet to make fun of her, not to have fun with her. I didn't like her. No audience enjoys watching an actor play a character the actor doesn't like. First, it's boring. Second, it's boring. Third, it's boring. If the actor doesn't like his or her character, don't ask the audience to like them.

There is no greater challenge for an actor than playing a villain. Most audiences love villains. In the old melodramas, hisses and boos were standing ovations for the actor. Acting 101: Find something to love in the character you play. It would take years before I acknowledged the maternity in my birthing of Harriet. I wrote her funny. I played her pathetic. Backseat hindsight.

The summer after *Ballroom* closed, I performed a new/old show in North Carolina. The show played for two weeks. The audiences would have been much happier with a *Hello Dolly* repeat. In expediency, I ignored Lily Tomlin's admonition to test the material. I was in a rush to get out of Washington. I wasn't upset. I knew I was going to rewrite the show when I found an off-Broadway theatre. It would be easier this time because I had credentials. I had been in that gorgeous flop *Ballroom.*

I found the struggling No Smoking Playhouse bordering Hell's Kitchen in NYC. The theatre was housed in a failed church of some denomination. The theatre founders converted the altar into a stage. A perfect homage to the Gods. From the beginning of time, religion and theatre had much in common. B.C., before Christ, various altars around the world were home to performances of all kinds, including human sacrifice. To this day, some theatre critics still practice human sacrifice every time they write a review.

I needed a place to stay... on the cheap. Over the years, I stayed in touch with one of my High School of Performing Arts buddies, a former crush, Conard. He was an empty-nester who lived in a large Upper West Side apartment. He offered me one of the bedrooms and told me to pay what I could. I was only there for half the week. So the price was right. Another performer had the other bedroom. I do recall Conard had a problem with roaches. Someone told him lizards were better exterminators than exterminators. One evening, while looking for the light in the bathroom, I stepped on the tail of Lizzie, the exterminator. Her tail came off. I was inconsolable until one of my mates explained the tail grows back. Another animal kingdom miracle. I was living the dormitory life I had skipped after high school.

Opening night of *Starting in the Middle* was more of a challenge than usual. Richard decided to attend. He played the producing Cecil Be DeSchwartz role to perfection. Dianne was safe, far away in China. Lori was in NYC, so I hired her to work the big spotlight that followed me on the stage.

Pamela, a senior in high school, created the real drama of opening night. Hours before the curtain went up, she called from D.C., insisting I come home immediately. After years of avoiding direct confrontations on the subject of career vs. motherhood, Pammy, who always had a great way with words but not a great sense of timing, demanded I come home. It wasn't that she didn't love me. She wanted a mother like her best friend had.

She sobbed. "Come home, now. I need my mother."

Here's what I should have said, "No matter what my mother or members of the PTA think, I am a mother first. I cannot do the show tonight. My daughter needs me. There will be no autographs after the show because I have to go home."

Here's what I did say, "Pamela, I love you. I will be home in three days. I'll buy those new sneakers you wanted so desperately—you know, the really expensive ones."

I watched as my rating dropped from bad mother to baddest.

With Pammy's tears in my ears, I can't say that I did a fully focused performance. I realize that any emotion that doesn't belong to the character an actor is portraying is a distraction and ultimately dishonest. Whether the character had guilt or not, she got guilt. Maybe that's why I never really liked most of my performances.

During the opening night party, Cecil B. De Schwartz worked the space like a pro. He found someone who he thought might further his wife's career. Richard introduced me to him. He had the most gorgeous head of white hair I'd ever seen. He also had the best damn smile. This man laughed. I could tell. His face held so many deep, deep laugh lines. I was intrigued. Richard handed me his card.

"Hey, Sal, this is Lee. He is an executive with a major network. He loved your show and wants to help you."

I looked at his card. I looked at him. He smiled. Very deep laugh lines. I smiled. He was just my height. You can't have everything.

"Call me."
"I shall."

No bells, whistles, or fireworks, but I knew a spark when there was a spark.

Once home, I bought Pammy her new sneakers. Detente! I could buy a million overpriced sneakers, but I would still be the baddest mother who chose career over her children.

I bought a pair of flats and called Lee.

This was no casual call. The little girl who danced in front of an open window, imagining agents, producers, and casting directors walking up and down her street watching her, had grown up to be an older lady telephoning a television producer who was waiting on the other end of the line to make me his star. I never understood why that telephone wire didn't explode and blackout New York City.

Our first evening together was filled with mixed signals. This happens when there is more than one track making a circuit around my brainball. One year before, Lee had lost his wife of thirty-three years. I was heartbroken for him. He corrected me. It was a very unhappy marriage. He wanted to divorce her many times but didn't because of the family. He admitted he would never have divorced her because he feared the consequences. Her death left him with a ton of guilt. Was that a warning signal? I continued with my not-so-hidden agenda. Lee, with his connections, would somehow rescue me from a fate worse than death... living in Washington, D.C., in a marriage that had run its course.

That first dinner held a frisee of sexual tension between us that was utterly divine. Lee had no wife. Richard broke his promise. There was no traffic on the road ahead. Our affair was the easiest one of the many I had had. No hotel bookings. He had his own spacious apartment in a ritzy doorman building on the Upper East Side. I looked past the shag carpeting. Shag carpeting? It was the '80s. Who did shag carpeting? Twin beds in the master bedroom told a story I knew only too well. Someone didn't want to have sex with someone. I enjoyed sex with Lee. So what if the wife had a suburban woman's taste? They had raised their family, two older girls, and a college-age boy, in Westchester while belonging to a Jewish country club. But who's making judgments?

It was obvious to me that I arrived just in time to save Lee from suburban purgatory. The pillow talk was wonderful. Helpful career conversations and having mutually good sex... fantastic. Obviously, not at the same time. Out of gossamer and butterfly wings, I created the greatest love story ever told. I was content. Lee was not.

In opposition to what I thought was every man's desire, no commitment, Lee was unhappy. He felt diminished by Richard's position as the husband.

Sharing me with Richard was impossible for him. That's how much he loved me.

Officer, I swear, I never saw the other car.

31

The Not-My-Fault Divorce

Marriage is the perfect foundation for a good divorce.
~ Harriet Ferment

Anyone who has ever experienced a divorce knows it is right up there with death. In fact, it is a death.

It came as a complete surprise to me when two out of three of my children decided that, without a doubt, this was a my-fault divorce. The elevator of my subconscious was still out of order. I didn't understand why they didn't understand; for their sake, I had sacrificed my career and stayed married to their father. Dianne, Lori, and Pamela thought if they had adjusted to their parents' operatic, in-technicolor arguments, why couldn't I?

If I were to be honest, which I make an effort to be on certain days of the week, the girls were more upset after the divorce because Richard and I never did truly divorce. Oh, to be sure, we went through the legal mumbo-jumbo of a divorce. We signed papers. Sold the house. Divided furniture and loyalties. Discontinued any physical intimacy. But we never cut the umbilical cord that was attached from the day of our marriage to his death. This was very confusing for any future partner for either of us.

Me to Lee, "Of course, I am divorced. But first, I need to check this out with Richard."

Richard to his many girlfriends and eventually his wife Beth, "My ex-wife is my best friend. Any problem?"

During the years of practicing open marriage, I had always chosen inappropriate and unavailable men. It was less complicated. Before Lee, Richard and I accommodated each others' needs and passions. No reason to contemplate divorce. Suddenly, the stars aligned, and all the conditions that had made divorce unthinkable evaporated.

Dianne, Lori, and Pamela needed to have one, if not two, feet out of the house. Check.
My mother needed to be dead. Check
The promise of no more extra-marital hanky panky had to be broken. Check.
Someone had to be waiting in the wings. Double Check!

I had almost given up on the last condition ever happening. Seriously, I didn't imagine anyone taking me seriously.

Waiting in the Wings, Man Wanted: Well preserved for her age, aggressively competitive, pathologically insecure, and guilty, mother of three adult children, wife of a successful businessman whom she helped make a successful businessman looking for a tall male with show business connections to make me a star. Must have low blood pressure.

The stars aligned enough for me to surrender to Lee's demand. I asked Richard for a divorce. At first, he balked. Not so much because he would miss me, but his business was at a difficult transition. His business was and always would be at a difficult transition. At some point, it dawned on Richard that a divorce would mean he wouldn't have to pretend he was single. He could take out his own personal ad.

Woman Wanted: A very successful businessman with a slow-growing paunch; a real bachelor; three adult daughters; helped former wife with her career; love theatre and sex; former full-time workaholic, now a less full-time workaholic.

The girls responded in kind to the divorce. Dianne had always threatened to run away if we divorced. She ran away to China before the divorce and stayed in China after the divorce. Lori, upon hearing about the divorce asked me what took me so long. Pamela believed in a second act yet to be written where her mother remarried her father, and we all lived happily ever after.

Divorce negotiations proceeded. We both used the same lawyer, our mutual friend Sam. The divorce was between Richard and me, not the girls. Richard would have a home for them in Washington. I would have a home for them in NYC. Richard would continue to support them financially. I would continue emotionally and psychologically supporting them if and when they allowed it.

The drama queen in me blew this divorce out of the park. In an act of bogus bravura, throwing myself into financial penury, I announced I wouldn't take any part in Richard's extremely successful and still growing business.

Instead I insisted that somewhere, somehow, Richard had to make some kind of mention of my presence and support for all the years leading up to his success. I suggested putting my 8x10 glossy atop a marble column at the entrance of the building. He would agree to anything as long as it didn't involve sharing in his business. Sam, our friend the lawyer, suggested Richard print a stock certificate indicating if the company ever made a stock option offer, as a former "employee," I would come into a portion of Richard's shares.

I asked, "Does it have my name and the company's name on that certificate?"
"It does."
"Where do I sign?"

32

It's So Nice To Have You Back Where You Belong

H ello, Sally!
I promised I would return. And I did.

I was back. I found an apartment I could afford — a fifth-floor walk-up studio. Good friends built me a loft bed because there was not enough room for a regular-sized bed. There was no closet, so I hung a rod beneath the loft bed to hang my clothes. My suitcase and my ever-ready three plastic bags served as my bureau. I had a bathroom. I just couldn't turn around in it.

Ask me if I cared. I didn't. For the first time in my 46 years, I had a room of my own. And if you think I didn't memorize Virginia Woolf's book, think again. She and her books were a major influence in my life. What a woman! And her husband, Leonard Woolf, with his care and concern for his wife and her work, was the blueprint I pasted onto every male I was ever interested in. No one ever came close.

My career was blooming. On some level, I must have taken it as a sign that though the girls, except for Lori, were unhappy because of the divorce, the yoke of guilt around my neck was looser. I was auditioning all over the city, and I was chosen for jobs off-Broadway, on Broadway, on television, and in movies. I didn't have any name the movie and television casting people could attach NYC credits to, but on the strength of that strong physical presence, I was cast in what I called blink parts. Blink, and you'll miss me. I was a middle-aged actress with a strong physical presence who played judges (*Law and Order* and *Night*

Court) - my daughters called that typecasting - Editors of newspapers (*The Paper*), busybody aunt (*Tiger Warsaw*), Fashion Magazine Editor (*Tatoo*), and shopper at Bergdorf Goodman (*So Fine*).

I also unpacked the one-woman show which was more and more oriented to exploring the yin and yang of Harriet Ferment. I found a fantastic new musical director, Robert Bendorf. Not only was he a fine musician, but he was a brilliant composer and lyricist. We would talk about a subject or issue that was uppermost in our minds – relationships, the failure of new relationships, and the next day, I would have a new song - *Revolving Doors, I Want To Be A Victim*. Bob was a contemporary composer who had a satirical and lyrical quality. He was a gay man in the '80s, and I was a divorced woman with children and a lover. We understood each other completely.

After years of waiting for the other shoe to drop, Lee's love and support made me feel safe and secure. Slowly, I lowered my protective shield. All those things I had to do or say to keep my motor running didn't seem so necessary — no more affairs. No more pretending. No more lies or fake orgasms.

I wasn't on duty 24/7. I could focus on my work. I hadn't done that since high school and college. When I walked into an audition, I was fully present in my mind and body. As I auditioned, I no longer had to calculate whether the next train to D.C. would get me back in time for one of the girls' events or worry about whether Lori remembered to defrost dinner. I'm not whining. It's the toll one pays on the road to stardom. The divorce and move to the city made it easier and the guilt lighter. And I was getting jobs. If I kept moving in the direction I was going, I could see buying my own dinner soon. For the moment, I was a little like Blanche Du Bois in *Streetcar Named Desire*, dependent on the kindness of strangers.

33

What is it About Second Anniversaries???

I mentioned that my musical director and friend Bob wrote a song about failed relationships called *I Want To Be A Victim*. His last love left him. I tried to console him.

"Bob, it sucks. It really does. How crazy is it to say you love someone one minute and leave them the next? My friend Marj is right. The truth will set you free. But first, it pisses you off."

I could give him this oh-so-wise advice because of how well things were going with me and Lee. During our first year, as the divorce proceeded, he was grateful. I was auditioning and getting jobs. He met the girls. They were sad about the divorce, but they really liked him. I thought his children were a minor hiccup.

One married young woman, one unmarried young woman, and one college-age boy, all adults. They didn't like me. The wife/mother was dead. I was always going to be "the other woman." I was the polar opposite of their mother - a lovely, unassuming suburban housewife. I was this opinionated, larger-than-life persona who knew what was best for everyone. I expected them to see beyond all that to my real heart. The heart that out of love for their father, I had left my husband of 27 years.

Early in our relationship, I had invited Lee's single daughter, Joanne, over for dinner at her father's apartment. We huddled in the kitchen to discuss the menu. She emphasized how much her father loved onions. Really? Oh, well, then I'll prepare something wonderful like a gorgeous thick and steaming onion soup with a mint apple salad to offset the oniony taste. Joanne was wonderful. She helped me prepare everything. She even set the table.

Lee arrived home. He was so happy to see his favorite daughter and his new love chattering away in friendly banter. I praised Joanne as the perfect kitchen partner. I brought out the fresh baguettes and steaming onion soup. Lee took one sniff.

"Is this onion soup?"
"Yes!"
"I hate onions."
"You hate onions?"

Joanne was in the kitchen. She came out with the apple mint salad.

"I tried to tell Sally-Jane you didn't like onions. She insisted you'd like this onion soup. But she also made a great apple mint salad. And with the bread and butter and the napoleons I bought for dessert... we'll be fine."

This was how it was going to be. I would always be the competition for their father's love and attention. If I was more secure... mature, would I have been so threatened by their open hostility? I don't know. All I did know was that I was desperate for his children to love me. What I didn't know then was that it was never going to happen. I don't think Lee or I saw what was coming. We were too busy writing and living the perfect romance.

We didn't know each other. So what? We were in love... the ultimate oxymoron. In those first two years, we traveled all over the world. We laughed and cried at the same plays, concerts, operas, and movies. We were sexually and otherwise completely compatible. I was happy to entertain his industry colleagues in his luxurious East Side apartment. Contacts and connections were important for both of us. He was in the biz. We talked for hours about my career moves and choices. I made passing suggestions and judgments on career moves for him, but most of our conversations were about me. It's hard to change a zebra's stripes or a leopard's spots, especially if you're not a zebra or a leopard.

In Lee, I finally found the personal manager and producer whose sole purpose in life was to make me a star. I didn't need to tell him this. He knew. Knowing and providing what your loved one desires is the definition of unconditional love. It says so right here in the Bible I wrote.

34

The Other Shoe Dropped

I have never felt better in my whole life. Except when I breathe."

~ Harriet Ferment

In a small Off-Broadway theatre on 42nd Street, I was performing in a new play, *Amidst The Gladiolas*. I had a good part. I played the wife of a dead policeman who, at his wake in a funeral parlor in Brooklyn, meets her husband's mistress. Interesting plot and characters. Enough to get some notice from audiences and critics. Ron, my director, was excellent. He challenged me and did it in a way that made it seem like I had thought of it. The best way. A year or so after the show closed, he became one of my closest friends. Don't ever let anyone tell you as a female, you can't have a male best friend, especially if sex is not involved. You can do it with sex as well, but it's better without it. Years later, I brought the subject up.

I asked him bluntly, "Are you my friend because you want to have sex with me?"

Just as bluntly, he replied, "None of your business".

The run was extended, but like most theatres, on and off Broadway, there were no performances on Thanksgiving.

This was to be my first Thanksgiving after the divorce – my first Thanksgiving away from the home where I had celebrated every holiday for the last twenty years. Yeah, this was big.

Maybe Lee and I and the girls could find a family restaurant and create a different kind of Thanksgiving. It wouldn't be the same for sure. But that wouldn't necessarily have to be a bad thing.

First, my daughters informed me they would be spending the holiday with their father. The man who was never there? Are you kidding me??? I stopped myself from saying anything. I had spread enough guilt for a lifetime. Time to suck it up. And I did. Until...

Lee's children convinced him they wanted to go to a family friend's Thanksgiving dinner... without me. He didn't have the courage or the courtesy to tell me in person. He called to inform me. I was shocked into silence. I imagined Lee had told his hosts if I wasn't going, he wasn't going. Figuring out what I imagined someone said and what actually was said was sometimes more than I could handle.

On the day itself, I thought I was doing quite well. I convinced me I was fine. The hell with everyone! I'm going to get through this just fine. No problem.

As the hours passed, my heart began palpitating, and I struggled to breathe. Short version - I went nuts. The man for whom I divorced my husband of 27 years had just abandoned me.

The righteous Gods of every religion gathered. It was time to punish me for not only the sins I had already committed but also for future sins yet to be committed. The pain was relentless and unforgiving. I was three years old again. Any minute, I was going to disappear. The walls made a good handball court for my head. I tore at my hair, making me look more and more like an insane version of that crazy hair lady comedienne, Phyllis Diller. I screamed until my vocal cords hurt. I cried so hard I couldn't catch my breath. Where was my brother David? Where was Richard? Dianne? Lori? Pammy? Bastard liars.

I was alone. This time, I was definitely going to disappear.

The doorbell rang. OMG! Somebody loves me. I ran to the intercom and pressed the button to speak,

"Who is it?"
"Floral delivery"

I pushed the button and let him in, thinking that if Lee thought a stinking bunch of flowers was going to make up for his betrayal, he was as crazy as me. I opened the door and received the flowers. They were gorgeous. I asked the guy why he was delivering on the holiday. He mentioned that his boss charged a lot of money to deliver on holidays, so it was worth it. This was his last delivery. He was excited. He was going home to a family Thanksgiving. I tipped him anyway.

I removed the card from its envelope. "Mumsy loves you. Marj"

The only person aware I was alone and who reached out to comfort me on my first Thanksgiving after the divorce was a new acquaintance who didn't know me at all.

I had met Marj through one of Lee's colleagues. She was a unique, attractive, older, crazy lady with a brilliant tongue that had no boundaries. Her thoughts and opinions were profound, profane, and outrageously funny. If I was an XL, she was XXXLLL. I met her the year before at Lee's company Halloween party. There were plenty of suits and expensive cocktail dresses. Marj was the only one to arrive costumed. She wore a leopard-spotted leotard with a hand-held swishing tail, topped by a cat's ears headband. I made fast tracks to meet her. It was love at first sight.

That insane Thanksgiving, she knew it was time to send in the cavalry. I blew my nose. Dried my eyes. Brushed my hair. Returned furniture to its place in the room and took some very deep breaths.

A few hours later, Lee called to tell me he was coming over. I don't remember what I might have said to him. I just knew I had received the first of many surprises to come in our relationship. The first being that Lee was not who I thought he was.

The reel that was playing the movie we were writing about our romance tore at the two-year mark. I had divorced Richard for Lee. I really hadn't. But I wasn't ready to acknowledge that. I needed my pound of flesh.

In my headball, Judas was a piker next to Lee. It's life-affirming to be with someone more guilty than you are. If I was surprised by the depth of Lee's betrayal, he was surprised by my pathological insecurity. It's something few of us would admit to, right?

Hello there! I am pathologically insecure. I need assurances and affection for at least eight hours every day. It doesn't have to be consecutive, which is a good thing. However, I am needy most of the time, which is a bad thing.

You know what? I was from Venus. He was from Mars.

After that Thanksgiving, I had no compunction returning to familiar territory. For the next thirteen years, Lee became part of a permanent menage et trois with Richard. I was never physically intimate with Richard again. That part of our relationship was well and truly over. If I felt unsure and insecure because Lee was unsure and insecure or if he chose his children over me, I gave myself permission never to be abandoned again. Like Lauren Bacall in a Humphry Bogart movie, I put my lips together and blew. Richard, still unmarried, returned to the field of play.

35

The Struggle of the Juggle

T hroughout most of the '80s, I became a master juggler. I juggled my relationships with Lee and Richard. I juggled my career and my children.

While I was in *Ballroom*, I became good friends with Sarah, our company manager. We'd commiserate for hours about men. There was a good reason men didn't birth babies. They may all want to look like Tarzan swinging from a vine, hands beating on their chests, giving their all to the call of the jungle, but give them an hour of labor pain or a stinky diaper to change, and there'd be a drastic population decline.

Sarah had an added problem. Her partner was a drug addict. She attended Al-Anon meetings at least four times a week. When she told me her man had stopped using and joined Narcotics Anonymous, I was thrilled for her.

"Now you can stop going to Al-Anon."
"Are you kidding? I have to go every day now."
"You're free. He has his own program."
"Sally-Jane, I spent my time at meetings whining and bitching about his sniffing and snorting. Now that he is in his own program and in recovery, it doesn't feel right to complain about his using when he isn't using. I need to focus on myself. How and why did I always choose destructive relationships?"

LIGHTBULB!

I accompanied her to her next Al-Anon meeting and found myself in a room of disparate folk with stories that were so similar to mine I was freaked out. As they shared, the pattern of my relationships became clear. As long as I focused on what Richard and Lee were doing, I never saw where the quarter they pulled from behind my ear came from. It didn't take long for me to see I had a problem. I was an addict. A relationship addict.

I was almost 50 years old and still living and making decisions based on childhood lies and fantasies. No matter how I thought I was succeeding, the balls I was juggling kept dropping.

Meanwhile, the riverside in downtown NYC was home to the beginning of the West Side Highway. New city housing was being developed. The units were rent-stabilized, making them actually affordable for a struggling menopausal actress. If I cycled my bills as I used to do before Richard hit the jackpot, I might be able to afford a two-bedroom, two-bathroom apartment - the first home I'd have for the girls since I divorced Richard.

In early 1982, the rental authorities contacted me to say the building was completed and the apartment ready. When they looked at my financials, they informed me I needed to provide a guarantor. Duh! My sole possessions were my three plastic bags and the contents within. I was a divorced woman who supported her bank with her overdraft fees.

In desperation, I called Richard and asked if he would guarantee my rent - not pay it - guarantee it. He hemmed and hawed, eventually agreeing. Richard was still my security blanket. He loved it. I didn't. Scenes of my mother begging her father for money flashed through my brainball.

With my hands filled with three plastic bags, I walked across the West Side Highway. The forceful wind tunnel formed by the confluence of the Atlantic Ocean and the Hudson River swept my hair and clothing all over the place, always threatening to blow me off my feet.

I had a two-year lease. I could buy a bureau and throw away those overworked plastic bags. Giddily, I hopped over the mud and cement of the ongoing construction site, waved hello to the whistling construction workers as they acknowledged my deft dance over potholes and other debris, and set up house on the 23rd floor overlooking the Hudson River. One morning at 6:00 am, the humongous Cunard liner, Queen Elizabeth, sailed up the river before my eyes. I opened the windows and started shouting to the passengers.

"Yoo Hoo! Up here! 23rd floor. Hey you! Can you see me? I see you. Yoo Hoo!"

I called friends, begging them to hurry over before they missed this glorious sight.

"Hurry up. Queen Elizabeth is cruising by my window. She is gorgeous. So close I can touch her."

I shouted and waved to the passengers on the top deck. They returned my wave. At least, I thought they did. Spectacular. I was so happy. Not all my choices turned to dust.

I did my next Broadway show, a revival of *The World of Sholom Aleichem*, playing opposite funny man Jack Gilford. Another show fraught with production problems multiplied by ego problems. So what? That's the nature of the beast. Or so I tried to convince myself. I was acting in a show on Broadway. My dream come true, right? If that was so, then why was I so unhappy? Every performance of the eight performances a week was a drag. I couldn't wait for my days off. It all came pouring out in a therapy session. I didn't want to do eight shows a week. I didn't want to perform in someone else's version of a good show that wasn't a good show. I was becoming a middle-aged judgmental curmudgeon.

The World of Sholom Aleichem closed. Phew. I was shuttling back and forth between Lee and Richard. It was exhausting. Lori was on a mission to find herself working at a radio station in Fairbanks, Alaska. I actually thought about joining her. Maybe that's what I needed: a deep freeze. Pamela was loving college and a new guy, Joel, who, from all appearances, was the real thing. We saw each other frequently for dinner.

Dianne was going to school and living in China. I rationalized. Dianne was very far away. I missed her. Just because she never said or wrote that she missed me didn't mean she didn't. What kind of a mother ignores her child's needs? What kind of a mother would cash in her last life insurance policy to buy a round-trip ticket to someplace halfway around the world? A mother who had made some grievous choices and was itching to get out of town.

I left for China.

36

ChinaTune

For those who have been to China in the last twenty years... fuggetaboutit! China in 1982 was not just the other side of the world; it was the other side of the moon.

In 1972, the Nixon administration negotiated a one-eyed peek into Chairman Mao's previously closed doors and windows policy. By 1982, that peek had morphed into travel visas and educational exchange programs, i.e., Dianne's language studies in Beijing. The difficulties I faced arranging my trip put me wise to the many problems I would face on my arrival in China. The processing and interviews at the Chinese Embassy took months. The final visa approval, which took several interviews, was only the tip of the iceberg, warning me in advance of the Chinese fear and suspicion of every foreigner. Knowing the history of abuse and power grabs by most of the major Western countries, it is understandable.

Twenty hours to Tokyo and another four hours to Beijing gave me plenty of opportunities to practice some Chinese phrases with Chinese passengers. It's nice to be able to say hello, goodbye, thank you in the language of the country you're visiting, but it is imperative to be able to ask for the bathroom.

Slowly, I realized I was heading into a world where, no matter what I did or how many words I learned, West was never going to meet East.

I discovered a bigger problem. It was 1982, and no one spoke English... except my daughter. It was as if one moment Dianne and I were waltzing in one direction, and suddenly someone yelled *REVERSE*! In a blink, our roles reversed. Dianne was the mother. With thumb in mouth, I was the daughter.

In a voice strikingly like her mother's, she barked, "You need to follow me or else."

I couldn't make a move without her permission. I didn't realize what a good memory Dianne had. Every slight, every insult, every negative, everything I had perpetrated on this child was returned. Where did she learn to be so judgmental?

I was forced by her arrangements to sleep communal style in the university dormitory. Privacy is for Capitalists. Most difficult for this Westerner with beginning knee problems was using Asian toilets. The physics of Western toilets was obviously omitted from How-to manuals for Chinese builders. They were always out of order. I learned to squat. Pushing forward the date of my knee replacements.

I was sorely in need of succor. The only international telephone was located in the University library. Twice a week, on certain days and times, foreigners were allowed to call home. Once a week, I called Richard. Once a week, I called Lee. Collect. I wouldn't have been able to afford any other kind of call, so I, for one, was grateful the Chinese phone system was as backward as its toilets. My once a week collect calls from Beijing to Washington, D.C., and Beijing to New York City saved my life.

"She left me in Mao's tomb today. She thought I was right behind her... I know... I know... No, I can't leave. She might think something is wrong."

We foreign devils were called gweilos, always pronounced with a snarl in the voice and a sneer on the face. Much of my time with Dianne was spent watching her as she navigated and worked in this alien world. She astounded me. By the time I arrived, Dianne was fluent in reading, writing, and speaking Mandarin. She developed friendships with Chinese students and teachers living and working in and around Beijing. Most of the time, she spoke Chinese because most of her time was spent with Chinese friends. She had no foreign accent. Ordering shoes in a store one day, a clerk asked if she was one of those Albino Chinese he had read about. She was an attraction wherever she went because she was this little blonde white girl who spoke and acted like a native.

I watched in awe as she fearlessly adapted to her new environment. Her Chinese friendships were suspect and, with any Chinese male, absolutely forbidden. She had already been detained by the people's police a few times. I didn't know it at the time, but while in China, I often was her beard for clandestine meetings with her Chinese boyfriends.

My visa was good for four weeks. We had just concluded two of those weeks in and around the environs of Beijing. Dianne's plan was to spend the last two weeks traveling to other parts of China. Those places she thought interesting and important for our mutual edification. The trip would end in Shanghai, where I was to fly back to New York City. She would return by plane to Beijing to continue her studies at the language school. Life is what happens while you're making plans.

Our itinerary was to begin with a train ride from Beijing to Xian. Dianne allocated a day to buy our tickets. In 1982, you didn't buy a ticket in China. You negotiated for one. Before buying any kind of ticket, you needed to prove you were not an enemy of the State. The ticket seller was part MI 6, CIA, KGB, and a prototype for an important Chinese national characteristic. Save-The-Face is to the Chinese what Savoir Faire is to the French, Stiff Upper Lip is to the British, loud and short-tempered is to the Americans.

Saving face is not a quick fix. It took hours to convince the ticket seller she wasn't an American spy. At an appropriate moment in the negotiation, she brought me over to the ticket booth, whispering to me to play confused and infirmed. Bowing her head, she mumbled in perfect Mandarin that she was a worthless but dutiful daughter honoring her old mother's last request to see the warriors of Xian before she died. If nothing else, the Chinese venerate the elderly.

We got the tickets.

I was excited. We were on our way to Xian, known for its recently unearthed collection of life-sized terracotta sculptures depicting the armies of the first Emperor of China, Qin Shi Huang. The Emperor had them sculpted and placed in his tomb for protection in the other world.

We boarded the train. Dianne neglected to tell me a few things. In her continuing challenge to live the life of the Chinese people, she booked Hard Seat tickets for the both of us... literally, a hard bench for a 705-mile journey from Beijing to Xian on a train that was built in the middle of the 19th century, which is why it took thirty-three hours to get there. Thirty-three hours on a hard bench. What else did she forget to tell me? Oh, yes, for most of the trip, to practice her new language, she was going to walk through the train speaking Mandarin. She would return periodically to our hard seat when it was time to eat.

Dining car service was not available for hard seaters. Not to worry. Food service was frequent and varied. Every time the train stopped at any crossroads or town, someone opened the windows and there before my tired eyes and aching back, pushcart chefs waited to serve the train's population. Their regional delicacies were displayed on their push carts, ready for purchase.

I wasn't ordering the American version of Chinese food at a local restaurant. However, once tasted, I knew I was being served fresh, seasoned, healthy food, and I was a happy camper. Dumplings of every stuffed variety, steamed or fried. I always had Dianne buy extra in case she didn't make it back to our bench. *Dumped Without a Dumpling* is not a headline I wanted to read. I don't like rice, particularly. I loved every rice dish I managed to get into my mouth. Losing much of it as I tried to navigate chopsticks. Pancakes rolled around ingredients I defy anyone to name. I ate frequently and heartily during my month in China, and here's a howdy-do... I lost weight. Value, not volume, whatever the hell that means.

I watched, again in admiration, as Dianne studied each cart and then proceeded to join in the chorus of hungry travelers yelling orders from the train windows. It was a cacophony that brought back memories of rush hour in the subways of New York – except it was all in Chinese with English subtitles provided by Dianne. The chefs cooked to order on their gerrymandered pushcart stoves, handing the food back to us through the train window. Anthony Bourdain would have gone crazy. Me? I didn't give a fig or a fortune cookie for these culinary delights. Sell me a cushion to save my ass, literally, and I'll chop your suey anytime.

Stopping at these little towns and crossroads to feed the masses and provide commerce to the local native population was very interesting, but it also afforded me an up-close look at the local populations.

Periodically, Dianne would return to see if I was still where she had left me. Actually, I can be more specific. She returned whenever it was time to eat. On demand. Just like when she was a baby. Her language abilities ordered our food. My yuan paid for it. It seemed like a fair exchange. It wasn't. I didn't mind paying. That's what parents are for, right? But I wasn't the parent. She was! I was the kid sitting on my hard seat, and by then, my seat was pretty damn hard, swinging my legs, thumb in mouth, waiting for permission from my mommy for everything. I was surrounded by suspicious Chinese. They never really took their eyes off me. I love people. Potentially, people were my next audience. But this was a hard, hard-seat crowd. They were not about to be charmed by this gweilo. I tried to do likable. I smiled until my cheeks froze. For the most part, I stared out of the window at the passing scenes.

In 1982, China was not a land of plenty. They had endured a famine not that many years before. With the opening of China came international cooperation and expansion for the farmers. They were once again plowing and harvesting their fields. But not with the latest equipment. I watched as farmer after farmer waded through rice paddies, guiding ancient plows pulled by gigantic water buffalos. The train moved so slowly I could see the details of their planting and harvesting. I'm a city girl. What did I know about agriculture? I knew enough to know I was witnessing ancient hand-to-hand combat with the land. I could see men, women, and children working the land, leather straps wrapped around their bodies extending to the ancient plows and attached water buffaloes as they dug deep into the dirt of the water-filled rice fields;

their small, thin bodies battered from back-breaking work. I watched the steady struggle from sunrise to sunset.

As the hours on the train clickety-clacked along, my body began to freeze up. I needed to move. I was alone on a hard bench on a train where many small Chinese people looked disapprovingly at this 5 '7" big blonde American.

Each hard bench comfortably sat four Chinese. I needed to save some of the seat for Dianne when she decided she was hungry. I needed every inch of my hard seat.

If I ever wanted to walk again, I had to move. I began to move my feet. In every dance class I ever took, the five positions of the feet were basic. Ignoring as best I could the harsh stares of my hostile audience, I put my feet through the familiar sequence: first position... plie... second position... plie... I tried to stay focused on my feet. I looked up and noticed a young woman seated across from me, watching. I moved my feet to another position... wait a minute! Did she just nod and smile at me? Third position... plie. I was not mistaken. The young woman *was* smiling at me. Seated, she began to mimic the five positions.

Was this a dream? Could it be? Was she a dancer?

It all began with nods and smiles and a repetition of movements. We were "talking."

We were both uncomfortable being watched. She for more specific reasons than me. What if someone decided to report her for fraternizing with a gweilo? We walked to the end of the car into the vestibule, away from critical eyes.

I would love to be able to relate the details of this sweet woman, but it was over 40 years ago, and what she looked like wasn't as important as who she was...my lifesaver. The first person in over fifteen hours to acknowledge my existence. She wore the standard Communist clothing - blue padded jacket with matching pants. I remember her hair was braided and circled her small head. No makeup. She smiled at me. The initial extending of a friendly hand – or I should say foot, brought me back to life.

My pantomime classes at school were useful. Without them, it would have been all smiles and dance positions. I was forging my own way into communicating... connecting... one human Westerner to one human Easterner. Whenever Dianne returned from her language extension course, she filled in the blanks about my new best friend.

It is definitely better to know the language, but however we did it, she and I communicated and made a connection.

Using our faces and our bodies and Dianne's translations, we exchanged our stories. My new friend was on her way to Xian to teach at the prestigious National Folk Dance School. Previously she was a touring performer with the National Folk Dance Company. Government policy required dancers to retire from touring and performing at a certain age to become teachers at the school. She was a performer. I was a performer. We had hours to pantomime playing charades with our stories until the other person finally understood. We arrived in Xian.

Chinese are not physically expressive people. They don't know from hugging. They definitely didn't kiss. I knew we would never meet again. I reached to give her a hug. In fear, she stepped back, and then, in a flash, we came together for a fast hug. She disappeared. She knew where she was going to be for the rest of her life. Some people might enjoy that kind of security. Not me.

I couldn't believe I would ever again get back on a train in China. But I did. A few days later, from Xian to Shanghai. Only thirty-one hours. But this time, I put my foot down. *No hard-seat.* When I entered the soft-bed compartment of that train, their version of First Class, six smoking communist commissars, took one look at this gweilo and immediately asked the conductor to change their compartment. It had nothing to do with sharing with a woman and everything to do with their suspected involvement with a foreign devil.

Hallelujah!!!!

It took over two hours to empty the compartment of the smoke from their cigarettes. For the next twenty-nine hours, I had a soft bed compartment all to myself. Dianne, still practicing her language, toured the train from engine to caboose. Periodically, we met in the first-class dining car for a meal or a "talk" with... other passengers, the conductor, waiter, chef. There was a lot to learn watching and listening to Dianne communicate and navigate this unfathomable world. If I didn't want to fall down the slippery slope I was on in China; I realized I needed to rework my attitude. I think it's called acceptance.

On arrival in Shanghai, I insisted on a hotel room with Western toilets. I opted for the renowned Peace Hotel on the Bund River. It hadn't been updated since the Japanese evacuated Shanghai thirty or more years before. Sensitive bathrooms periodically worked and then inexplicably didn't. Doors could be locked only some of the time. Chinese officials always needed access.

The bar at the Peace Hotel was the core of the hustle. Chinese musicians played their version of American Jazz. When I arrived in 1982, many of the musicians of the '30s, '40s, '50s were still playing their versions of Gershwin, Porter, Berlin, Rodgers and Hart. I had a hard time putting lyrics to whatever song they were playing.

I took two important side trips from Shanghai. First, I took a one-day trip to Suzhou, the city known for its magnificent garden villas. Then, I took a two-night trip to Hangzhou, subtitled "the Switzerland of China." It was a city of island lakes and pagodas, footbridges surrounded by weeping willows and blossoming trees.

Hangzhou changed my life. I was checking into a *hotel* that, amazingly, had been built centuries after the Great Wall of China. The plumbing worked. I found it interesting how stupid things like running water and toilets that flush made a hotel in China in 1982 feel like the Ritz. As I was checking in, my ears perked up. Was that a new foreign language I heard? It was... English. Two men using words I was distantly familiar with were also checking in. I understood what they were saying. OMG! It didn't take me two seconds. I raced over to their side of the desk and almost kissed them. I begged them to keep talking—music to my ears. Within minutes, we were best friends.

Peter and Andre were Australian cinematographers. Peter lived in Sydney, Andre in Hong Kong. We were all in the biz. This was a dream. After almost four weeks of being muzzled by a foreign language, like Vesuvius, I erupted. To this day, we really are still good friends.

On our last evening, we shared where each of us was headed. I had my return ticket from Shanghai to New York. Peter was returning to Sidney to film a movie. Andre suggested visiting Hong Kong and invited me to stay with him. He and his partner had plenty of room. I already had my ticket home.

"So what?"
"Easy for you to say."
"Hong Kong is known for having the cheapest flights to anywhere in the world. Cancel your ticket, and I'll put you in touch with a travel agent who will get you a flight to wherever you want to go—on the cheap!"

I wasn't sure I could afford it. For the first time since I arrived, I looked at my finances. Because my wonderful darling daughter dragged me no-class all over China, I had almost as much money as I had when I arrived. *Thank you, Mommy.*

I was off to see the Wizard... the wonderful Wizard of Hong Kong! With Peter and Andre's counseling — they thought I should do the Australian thing — I'd travel until my wallet was empty.

Just thinking about being someplace in the world and running out of money brought on a major anxiety attack. So, I did what I always did when that happened. It didn't happen.

This is almost my favorite part of my China trip.

The night before we were scheduled to return to Shanghai, I explained to Dianne that I was going to take a boat from Shanghai to Hong Kong. Andre had sailed the ship from Hong Kong to Shanghai and said it was fun and cheap. I was going to stay with Andre in Hong Kong. From there, I would figure out what to do next. I further explained it was because of her that I had enough money to be able to continue this adventure. I further, further said that if she wished for it, a new career as a travel agent for the physically and financially challenged awaited her. She was not happy. Like mothers before her, she waggled her finger disapprovingly at me.

"How can you stay with someone you don't know?"

OMG! Did she remember how many times, over the years, I had asked her the same question?

"He could be a sex maniac."

If only.

Andre was gay and had a partner. It'll come out in therapy somewhere why I didn't share that information with Dianne.

Before leaving Shanghai, our days together were good. Maybe because I was leaving, she was glad I came.

Standing on the deck of the luxury (ha!ha!) freighter as it pulled out of Shanghai, I was excited and terrified. The usual.

One thought comforted me...

Collect calls can be made from anywhere.

~~~

INTERMISSION

Until my invasion of China, I thought I knew who I was: a basic 1930s model of a middle-aged, middle-class divorced mother of three young adult women, actress/writer, attempting and ultimately failing to control her relationships with her former husband and on again/off again lover. As the former freighter converted passenger ship sailed out of Shanghai's harbor, I was dimly aware of this woman standing on deck waving goodbye to what appeared to be her daughter on the dock.

Interesting. There was definitely a resemblance. But it couldn't have been me. No way. I, who didn't go to the grocery store alone, would never begin a journey around the world by myself. I wonder what the Chinese put in their water.

~~~

"Life will break you. Nobody can protect you from that, and being alone won't either, for solitude will also break you with its yearning. You have to love. You have to feel. It is the reason you are here on earth. You have to risk your heart. You are here to be swallowed up. And when it happens that you are broken, or betrayed, or left, or hurt, or death brushes too near, let yourself sit by an apple tree and listen to the apples falling all around you in heaps, wasting their sweetness. Tell yourself that you tasted as many as you could."

~ Louise Erdrich, *The Painted Drum*

37

Around My World In the 80's

I didn't know it at the time, but Hong Kong was going to be the first stop on an unplanned world tour. Like the gift that keeps on giving, I began a tour that kept going on and on and on. Some of it was actual, physical. Some of it was virtual, emotional. All of it was life-changing.

On board my Chinese gambling ship, I met a lovely student backpacker from Yorkshire, England. If I was ever going to be in England, he asked me to call his mother and assure her he was well and still globetrotting. I took his mother's address but knew I was only going to Hong Kong to visit my new friend Andre and not to England.

The city of Hong Kong was fantastic. A brilliant mixed society with a unique geography. Mountains surrounded by the sea, the South China Sea. I was overwhelmed by the many different ethnicities. I was treated to a party on a Chinese junk. I couldn't wait to call Richard and/or Lee collect to tell them I actually jumped from a Chinese junk into the China Sea. I was doing a beautiful imitation of Esther Williams when someone aboard the junk yelled, "Shark!" That was my last dive into the South China Sea.

Hong Kong is an island surrounded by islands. One more exotic and interesting than the other. There are many Islands to visit by ferry. Lantau was the home of an ancient monastery. Thank goodness Andre went with me on this excursion. I was listening to a serenade of the gongs that came from the Buddhist Temple.

Suddenly, Andre yelled, "STOP."

Awakened from my sleepwalking, a few inches in front of me, a snake slithered across my path. Stop? Are you kidding? I froze. It continued on its way into the high grass. Andre sat down. Right there in the middle of the path. What was his problem?

"That was a cobra." I was a city gal. What was a cobra doing living outside its herbarium?

I sat down on the footpath next to Andre. We clung.

Andre was as good as his word. I was able to buy a ticket that flew me from Hong Kong to home via London.

In London, my good friends Fred and Marianne, who were former neighbors in Washington, D.C., welcomed me to their London home. I called the backpacker's mother, Ann, as I promised I would. She invited me to visit her in the countryside outside of York, adjacent to the mysterious moors. Ann was middle-aged, attractive, and lived alone in a thatched-roof cottage. It was hard for me to wrap my head around this charming woman living alone in a small cottage in a small village without a movie house adjacent to an area previously listed in my imagination as a horror film location. Think of *Frankenstein, Dracula, Wolf Man*. They were always out on the moors doing horror-movie things. We actually got into some good discussions. Not about horror movies. About living alone and how it was preferable to her than living with her son's father and other men in her life. I agreed more than I disagreed, but her ideas frightened me.

She lent me a walking map of the moors. Daily I would head out to explore different areas. I stepped on sheepshit all over the place. Wildflowers were blooming amid ancient rock formations, casting shadows as the sun set. There was always a fog that mysteriously moved in and out and gave me chills. Of course, I had to do the touristy thing. I never missed a chance to call,

"HEATHCLIFF??? I've returned."

Through Fred and Marianne, I met a wonderful woman named Charlotte. She had studied to be a concert pianist but discovered her talent was better suited to supporting artists rather than being one. She convinced me to come with her to Paris. Why not?

How refreshing it was to visit Paris without my honeymoon luggage strapped to my body and to stay in a hotel with an elevator. If I wanted to keep traveling, I had to get out of Paris. It was too damn expensive.

Isideros was one of Dianne's former boyfriends. Like her mother, Dianne never threw away any of her men. Before I left China, Dianne mentioned he was going to be at home in Athens for the summer. I collect called her for his number. He was thrilled to hear from me. I flew from Paris to Athens, where Isideros and his family hosted me for two days. Athens was home to my calling... the plays of Aeschylus and his brethren. The acoustics in the ancient but majestic amphitheaters were as good as they had been centuries ago. I went down to the stage and recited Emily's monologue from Thorton Wilder's *Our Town... Does anyone realize life while they live it? Every, every minute.* It was thrilling... thrilling.

I was finally tired of packing and repacking. I wanted to settle somewhere and open a leather-bound notebook I had with me and had yet to write anything in it. I wanted to take the time to commit my thoughts and words to paper. I wanted to stop and catch my breath.

Traveling alone by the seat of my pants was exhausting. I was forced to be dependent on the kindness of strangers. Without language, it was ridiculous. I hate fish. Do you know how many times I ordered fish when I thought I was ordering chicken? It always happened in a cafe that was small enough where the chef waited for the crazy American to laud his culinary skills.

First, I'd eat a piece of fish. Then, have a piece of bread. Eat another piece of fish. Have a sip of wine.

Without a nearby cat, I would have been done for. I ended the half-eaten meal with a brilliant pantomime of how full I was, signaling I couldn't possibly eat another morsel.

Why was I the crazy American? I was a single, middle-aged woman traveling alone. In the 80's in small towns in Greece, that's a crazy American.

In spite of my critical, judgmental self, I became aware there were other ways to be in the world. I was confronted with decisions others used to make for me. Fear of the unknown, fear of the known, you name it, I feared it. I was frightened of almost everything. Missing trains, buses, finding toilets, missing ferries, finding toilets, misunderstandings (so easy to do without language), finding toilets.

I remembered reading a mysterious and brilliant novel by John Fowles called *The Magus*. The setting was on the island of Spetses. I ferried over to Spetses and rented a room in the house of an island family. Our mutual language barrier made it difficult to expand beyond the *Yah-Su* (Hello). I didn't want to go any further than that. So I didn't.

There was only one problem... my money was finally beginning to disappear. China was cheap. Every place else in the world was not.

I had a daily routine. An early morning walk to the bakery for a roll and a big cup of tea with lots of sugar. Down to the beach or the woods to write for three or four hours (my room was much too hot to work in.) Skip lunch. After work, swim in the sea or walk around the island. Dinner time walk to a seaside restaurant for soup or a salad with lots of extra bread and butter. If I could, I saved some of it in a napkin for a lunchtime snack the next day. I was reduced to the kindness of a Greek waiter who surreptitiously left a plate or two or three of food along with a glass or two of red wine. All of which I was not unaware would eventually cost me.

Each day, I wrote. Each night, I pondered what other women over the centuries had deliberated. It seemed to me that, in return for favors, the smart ones walked away with diamonds and rubies and pearls. Some

Baba Ganoush or a slice of Baklava, my expected reward, didn't seem a fair exchange.

Onassis kept his small yacht (yeah, right) down by the dock. Not far from the public phone booth. What Greek Island didn't he own?

Collect call time. It was Richard's turn. I played the part of the mother of his three children. I was faint from hunger. I forgot. I *was* the mother of his three children.

Guess what. He was coming to Athens for a business meeting. The fickle finger of fate hit the jackpot. He asked me to meet him at the airport. I was really hungry. I asked if he could come sooner. The poor waiter was philosophical about wasting food on a no-show.

Richard arrived at the airport.
I ate.
He went to his meeting.
I followed him, waiting for my next meal.

His meeting was on a yacht docked in Rhodes. We departed for a cruise in the Aegean Sea. Spectacular. Richard and the wife of the couple who owned the yacht sat down in the salon of the boat to hash out some deal or other.

I sat on the deck with my notebook and continued writing my China saga, waiting for Richard to join me.

I waited.
And waited and waited.
Same ol' same ol'.

The owner brought the yacht to anchor near a tiny rock island that was noted for its butterflies. While the business deal was being negotiated, the owner's husband was going off on a trek through the island. I invited myself along. He was pissed. He wanted to be alone. Remembering China, I said that was fine. I was used to walking and talking to myself. We left the yacht. The boat, the deal makers, and the crew would meet us later on the other side of the rock.

What a day! The sun was shining, the wind was blowing, and my senses were overloaded by the thousands of colorful butterflies dipping and nestling for a moment on fields and fields of glorious wildflowers. I was lost in my own Fantasia. I sat comfortably on ancient boulders surrounded by butterflies fluttering all around me as I ate my buttered baguette and sipped from my bottle of water in my own Garden of Eden. The owner's husband, the snake, was out of sight and out of mind.

He avoided me. I kept my distance. I confess I kept one eye on him as the sun began to dip below the horizon. The wind picked up. Thank goodness I followed him because as the sun finished dipping, he was the only one with a flashlight. It was dark. There was no boat. He remained aloof. And if he didn't think losing me would lose the deal, I wouldn't be writing this.

Finally, the yacht came into view. We were on a rock. With the wind whipping up the water, the boat couldn't get close because of the rocks. I would have to jump. I thought maybe I'd wait till it was daylight. Not possible. The owner's husband said it was easy. He jumped. He fell onto the boat. "See? Easy!"

Everyone on deck was yelling encouragement. Easy when you were the one *not* jumping. The boat was bobbing up and down on the waves. I had had years of dance training. One of my favorite moves as we danced across the room was the big leap. Eyeing the gap between me, the rock, and the boat, I put myself back in that class and imagined I was Rudolph Nureyev's greatest rival. In that leap... in that moment... I flew blindly into the darkness.

It was literally a *leap of faith*.

Obviously, I did make it. Not so obvious was the next few days on board in bed and in the bathroom, emptying everything from every orifice.

I had escaped death. I was surprised. I was grateful. Richard was very sympathetic. Then he looked at his watch and returned to finish the deal.

We flew home. I stayed in NYC. He flew south.

I hadn't the slightest doubt. I was never going to remarry Richard or return to Washington, D.C.. But, as long as Richard would allow it, I would use him as my buffer against my ongoing insecurities around Lee.

I was in my fifties. I had met Richard when I was 18 years old. We had history. Not all of it great. Not all of it terrible. We shared three glorious daughters whom we loved... differently, true, but we loved them. Dare I say it without being hoisted on my own petard one more time: we loved each other. I'm not sure it was *ever* a romantic love. We found in each other a challenging, interesting, and moveable feast for twenty-eight and counting years. I really don't think either of us was willing to let the other go. And we never did.

After almost three months of wandering the world, I returned to NYC. My apartment contained my gaggle of girls. I couldn't stop squeezing, hugging, kissing. I was totally obnoxious. Dianne was on break from her classes. She was going back to China for another semester of school and a part-time job. The Far East was a siren call for Dianne. Lori was just settling in at college in Olympia, Washington. Pammy was entering her second year of college in New York City.

Once home, I kept circling my apartment, tearfully grateful for every little tchotchke that before I left I had been sorry I ever bought. Toilet paper and the environs of my American bathroom became my new place of worship. In foreign countries, I was embarrassed by American overconsumption. At home, it didn't take a minute before I was happily over-consuming.

It also didn't take a minute before I returned to my dance of the rivals starring Richard and Lee. There were times I would get a niggling feeling over the hairs on the back of my neck. Some people call that intuition. I didn't know I had any of that. I just called it a niggling feeling over the hairs on the back of my neck.

Lee once again chose to exclude me from his family Thanksgiving. Excluding me. I was heartbroken without going crazy. Forewarned is... is... is... forewarned, right?

All three of us were doing the same 'ole, same 'ole dance.

Someone had to find the exit sign.

38

Welcome to My Waterloo

I dove into reworking and rewriting yet another version of my one-woman show.

Lee made many business trips to London. I applied a healthy slice of Thanksgiving guilt. He took me with him on his next trip, where I began my search for a British producer.

Someone I met through Lee recommended a producer he had used. I called. We met. I made him laugh. While phones were ringing and business was being conducted, I performed my monologues. He was socoo British. He was uber-polite and wouldn't dream of interrupting me.

When I returned to the States, I offered, and he agreed to look at a tape I was going to make of the show. If he liked what he saw, he would produce the British version of my show. Stardom was just a skip over the pond back to the States. First The Beatles, soon Sally-Jane. I am always astonished at the lengths the human ego denies reality.

I begged, borrowed, and stole to make that tape. I took the Lily Tomlin tutorial seriously. I tried out new material, discovering what worked and what didn't work. I was doing all this writing and editing in New York, not London. I should have read Oscar Wilde more carefully; "England and America are two nations divided by a common language."

I sent the tape to London. Richard, the British producer, loved it. He booked a four-week run at a small theatre, which was in an extension of a drama bookshop in Hempstead. There was no way the girls –

Dianne in China, Lori and Pamela in college – would make it over to see their Mum. Claiming founders' rights, Richard would never miss an opportunity to tell the world he had discovered me. He would definitely fly over. Lee played cat-and-mouse about attending, though he was working next door in Paris. I was beginning to discover this adorable, funny, and sweet man had very strong passive-aggressive tendencies.

I didn't need a therapist to tell me my relationships were utterly predictable. I had married my mother. I had partnered with my father.

Richard, the producer, found a flat for me. He also found a talented musical director. He introduced me to Mary, an extraordinary publicist. She wasn't sure about taking on an unknown American, but I put any hesitation out of her mind. I forced her to watch my performance of the whole show acapella in her tiny office. What can I tell you? She loved crazy American people. To this day, she is still my very good friend, and we can bring each other to tears laughingly remembering our first meeting.

After my first trip to a British hairdresser in London a week before the opening, I should have packed my bags and flown out on the next plane to anywhere. The man doing my hair asked how I was enjoying London. I have never understood sotto voce.

What's not to like? London was fabulous. Its history, its culture, its Cockney taxi drivers. I further explained I was getting a distinct impression that British men didn't have a very high opinion of women. From the back of the salon, aglow with a head full of aluminum foil highlighting her hair, a woman rushed up and, in the poshest of the posh accents, educated me:

"No, dahling. You have it all wrong. You see, the British male is really only concerned with three things: His club, his job, his pet. He rarely thinks about women at all!"

I was in trouble.

Unfortunately, my friend Mary was very good at public relations. She convinced every reviewer who ever wrote for any paper or magazine to come to the show. Smaller papers and magazines gave me warm reviews. But all the major newspapers said the same thing:

She was funny, she had a good voice, she was a good actress, and thank goodness British women are not like American women.

I wanted to close the show, put my tail between my legs, swim home, and, if God was good, drown before I got there. The few warm reviews and an unknown director kept the run and me alive. This director had been in the audience opening night and came to the theatre the next day. As a Brit, he thought the show was good but needed reworking.

The Oscar Wilde quote about American English was a big problem in the script. Also, in the 1980s, not too many British women made fun of the male establishment. The saga of Harriet Ferment relentlessly pointed a finger at the hapless, non-thinking, non-feeling male in the person of Franklyn Ferment, Harriet's husband.

You are lucky, Harriet, to have a husband who has committed himself unselfishly to work like a dog for our future happiness and security. Sometime soon I will be able to come home for dinner. By that time, the mortgage will be paid off; I can refinance, amortizing the profit over thirty years to hold down on the capital gains. And that's how much daddy loves his little girl. We haven't done it for a week, Harriet. Could we do it tonight?

It was understandable that the British males were glad British women weren't like American women.

The Good Samaritan director thought I should continue.

I was splitting the cost of the production with Richard, my producer. I thought that was fair. After the reviews, Richard, the producer, and I agreed to continue paying the staff and the music director. If we didn't take any salary, the show could continue playing.

I only made one stipulation. If there were less than seven in the audience – the total number of crew and staff including myself – I would cancel the performance. It's some kind of an achievement for me that I only had to cancel once. Though I learned a great deal performing for eight or nine people, I would prefer never having to do it again. There were so few of them. They were so British. They were like my family whenever I performed. No reaction. They hid their laughter. Little titters behind cupped palms. "Veddy," polite applause. However, it was on those nights that one or two people ventured backstage to tell me how much they enjoyed the show. Go figure!

So much happened in those six weeks. The transformation of the show. Meeting Mary and her partner Barry, who never tired of watching me juggle Richard and Lee's visits. She was a great help ushering in one as the other left. My personal ménage à trois joined the many French farces that were playing in West End theatres.

After two lonely Thanksgivings, I admitted Lee was not dependable. Richard was not only a backer but he remained for the rest of his life, my security blanket.

It was time to pull the plug. I had squeezed the experience dry. Once more, I was out of money. I needed to go home, pound the pavements, get a job, and pay the rent.

If you are free of failures, you're not taking enough risks.

~ Laurence Olivier

39

California, Here I Come...

L ee accepted a new job in Los Angeles. Somewhere in my overworked imagination, I thought if we were away across the continent from his children, life would be different. Shame on me.

Our life in Hollywood began with an apartment that looked like a movie set. A large balcony overlooked the Pacific Ocean providing spectacular sunrises and sunsets for which I was very grateful as they were my only reality. We were both so skittish. Lee had only lived with one woman for thirty-three years. I had only lived with one man for 27 years. We didn't do well with either person. What the hell were we thinking?

Our checkered history and insecurities made our time together a waiting game. Which one of us was going to ignite the time bomb of incompatibility that was destined to explode?

The minute I unlocked the door stepping onto the movie set, I knew I had made a mistake... a big mistake. Where the hell was my escape route? In Brooklyn, there were so many windows to climb out of. I didn't need one married to Richard because most of the time, I was alone. This high-floor apartment provided brilliant views of the ocean, but only a Tarzan or Esther Williams could escape. I was stuck.

We had a year's lease... a year. I did what I always did. I pretended I didn't know what I knew.

I began the Los Angeles version of pounding the pavements. Driving my rental car and freewaying from one talent agency to another looking for the Starmaker. My lucky day, an agent from a well-known agency was in need of a younger Eve Arden type, a much-required character type in the sitcoms of the day. He signed me to a contract and began sending me out on auditions.

Surprisingly, I did find work in L.A.. Not the work I wanted to do. Most Hollywood casting directors went strictly for type.

"Hi! How are you? My name is Sally-Jane Heit, and here is my 8x10 glossy and my resume."
"You're so self-assured. This role is for someone who is very insecure."
"I understand. But as an actress I can play insecure very well. That's what actors learn to do. Play different emotions. As a matter of fact, I am feeling very insecure right now."
"Really? You don't look insecure at all. Next..."

It took me a while, but eventually, I realized that Washington, D.C., with its political focus, and Los Angeles, with its show business focus, were the sister cities in different businesses. Wherever I went, in either town, if I walked into an office or a party or a restaurant, eyes did an immediate scan... was I someone... no one... on the rise... in decline? It didn't take long for eyes to pass me over in search of bigger fish.

For all my emotional and career woes, there was one great compensation. The California geography. Not the mudslides, earthquakes, and fires, but the ocean, desert, and mountains were glorious. Lee and I covered as much territory as we could.

The girls made their way out to the West Coast for a visit. Dianne had completed her China tour and was working in NYC for a foreign policy think tank. Lori moved to Seattle to work for senior health care programs, ever more involved with a serious Rob. Pamela graduated college and she and Joel entered different law schools intending marriage upon their graduation.

My brothers Raymond and Allyn lived on the West Coast, and my sister Marilyn had three daughters in different places all over the state. I managed to connect with Marilyn's family. Family judgments by my mother had no sell-by date. A million years later, Raymond and his wife

Shirley, still carrying the mark of my mother's disapproval for eloping, kept a polite distance.

My brother Allyn, brilliant, mentally unstable with Parkinson's, before the development of dopamine, was terminally ill. A few visits, at this stage of his illness, could not bridge the gap. I was bewildered. We were part of the same family. They were my brothers. I didn't know them. How was that even possible?

During my year in L.A., I was going through the worst of my menopausal misery. Hot flashes??? Are you kidding???? While waiting to read at an audition, my makeup literally slid off my face. My moods ran from the silent treatment to Vesuvian eruptions. Lee lost patience with me. He accused me of having serious mental issues. I did. Everything from brain fog to a psychological and physical breakdown. I persuaded him to go with me to my gynecologist. She explained menopausal symptoms and conditions. He didn't believe her. He thought I wrote the script she delivered.

It wasn't a good time for Lee. On top of my volatility, Lee had job problems. He was the wrong fit for the organization he worked for. His family wanted, dare I say, *needed* him back East.

Most people believe money makes the world go 'round. Since I never had any, I wouldn't know. I had insisted on sharing some of the rent of our fabulous Hollywood digs. My small share afforded me a very small sense of independence, which I could ill afford. I have always had a healthy disrespect for money. In my limited experience, it was the excuse others used to control me. Whether it was my parents, Richard, Lee, or a waiter in Spetses, my survival depended on the kindness of others. Irrationally, I spent money as if I had it. I was in debt much of the time. I supported all my one-woman show expenses by acting jobs in theatre, television, and movies and resorted to passing the begging bowl when necessary. It was a precarious lifestyle.

Moving to California, even for a year, put me more financially behind than ever. I had to pay rent in two places. I tried to sublet one bedroom in my New York apartment, but I had to evict the tenant when I discovered she tripled my phone bill by calling her boyfriend somewhere in downtown Asia. As if that wasn't bad enough, he called her collect on my phone. Who would do such a thing?

My apartment in NYC was my safety net so moving out of it was not negotiable. When I think about how I knew from day one that California wasn't going to work, I was grateful I didn't cancel my lease.

Just as I thought life on the West Coast couldn't get any more complicated, Richard called. He wanted to fly to L.A. to present me with a check. Money? Richard was voluntarily giving me money? Get out the brass band. No, wait. Better than that, deposit the check in my account immediately before the next overdraft forces me to change banks again.

He insisted he needed to present it to me personally. I gritted my teeth, tightened my belt, and explained I was flying back to NYC for a special audition in a few weeks. We agreed to meet at my apartment.

As part of our divorce ten years ago, Sam, our mutual lawyer, had worked out an agreement that I had signed, giving me a small share of Richard's stock in his organization. When I signed it, Richard insisted the paper had no value. Maybe it had no value to him. To me, with my name on the certificate, it was clear without my presence, there would be no business. Ten years later, apparently, the situation had changed. The paper the stock was printed on did have some value after all.

He tried to explain about stock option plans and more business gobble-de-gook to which I stared at him incomprehensibly. In frustration, he gave up trying to explain and handed me a check for more money than I had or would ever again see in my life. Not telling... put me against the wall facing a firing squad... never telling.

Immediately, I burst into tears. Richard was moved. He gave me his clean handkerchief to dry my eyes. I still have it. He was glowing.

"I told you the reason I worked so hard and wasn't home all those years was for you and the girls. You never believed me." His puffed-out chest couldn't get puffier.

What is it about us humans? Why do we make it up as we go along? Silly questions. No need to burst his bubble of selfless achievement. The girls and I knew better. We would benefit from his hard work, but we were never the propeller of his obsession.

Breathing heavily through my tears, I cried, "Oh, honey, this isn't what I wanted."

I'm not sure he even heard me. It didn't matter. I was not going to refuse the money. And if I thought I would never have to worry about money ever again, I didn't know me at all. But we already know that.

In a blink, I had become a woman of independent means. I was not prepared. I had no frame of reference for paying bills on time. Pawnbroker visits were a regular part of my life when I had anything to pawn. Buying when I didn't have any money to buy – what the financial columnists called indiscriminate overconsumption– was in my DNA.

If having enough money was the panacea everyone thought it was, why wasn't I jumping for joy? Because after a childhood of living in someone else's clothes and a marriage of peddling bills to pay the mortgage and a divorce that left me beholden to the kindness of strangers. It took a while to register this new reality.

I was still out of it when I returned to the West Coast. I probably didn't do a great job of explaining to Lee what had happened with Richard. It really hadn't registered in any concrete form. I don't think it would have made any difference. Change for most of us is difficult. My new wealth, especially because it came from Richard, made our impossible relationship even more impossible.

Our one-year lease came to an end. Lee left his job. Unconsciously, we knew the experiment, which from the beginning had no chance of working, was over. We had arrived in Los Angeles with all our baggage. We had never unpacked it. I don't think we even discussed how over it was. We both knew. We were returning to the East Coast and our separate homes.

We decided to take the long route home, traveling up the West Coast of California, Oregon, Washington, Montana, driving north into and driving across Canada, eventually going south into New York State, finally landing in New York City. Together, we were apart.

40

Two Weddings and a Funeral

In the late '80s and early '90s, as Lee and I struggled to keep our relationship afloat, two of my daughters, Pamela and Lori, were heading for the altar.

Modern marriages and divorces created an overabundance of parents for the bride and groom. You needed an illustrated program to tell the real parents from the step-parents, and if there was more than one marriage and divorce in the parental parties, the family Bible didn't have enough pages.

Richard had met Beth.

I was happy for him. I really was. This happened before Lee and I moved to California while we were both still in our delusional state. I had Lee. Richard should have someone, too. Sometimes, I am so fair it hurts.

That "fairness doctrine" evaporated when Richard started making noises about marrying Beth. I explained to Richard that if he married Beth, the "we" we were would no longer be. Our calls and meetings with each other would be limited, if not impossible. He disagreed, further explaining he had already informed Beth that his relationship with me was a no fly zone area in their relationship. For him, my presence in his life would be non-negotiable for any future partner. Our postnuptial agreement.

Beth was a widow with four grown children. She was attractive, smart, engaging, smart, enterprising, and smart... she accepted the condition. From the beginning, she reached out in friendship because she was told to. I am an actress. I responded politely. The early years were filled with bumps and pitfalls as each of us adjusted to our new designations. Richard, aka Solomon, was having the time of his life. Over time, the trio achieved a relationship of warmth, admiration, respect, and, eventually, love. You're right! It's a Hallmark Channel Movie. We had particular fun when introductions were made.

"Hello, nice to see you again. This is Sally-Jane, my first wife. This is Beth, my present wife."

And for all those snickering at the first Mrs. becoming friends with the second Mrs., be my guest. Snicker away. It's a testament to how committed we were to our priorities. The children: hers, his, and mine. She loved Richard and cared for him brilliantly through his many health issues and illnesses. His relationship with me had to be a trial for her, which she handled with grace and fortitude. On some level, she must have known I was never going to be a threat to her. He loved her that was clear. I never wanted to go home again, ever. The mé·nage à trois was comfortable. My daughters were uncomfortable whenever an occasion brought the threesome together. What can I tell you? They were normal.

Pamela and Joel's bucolic wedding was Richard and Beth's first appearance as husband and wife. It made me a little nuts. All right, already! It made me a lot nuts. I only acted out a little. All right, already! Maybe a little more than a little. Maybe I bought a more expensive mother-of-the-bride outfit. Maybe I went to the hair salon and chose a more Monroe hairstyle and color. Maybe I went to Elizabeth Arden's for a facial makeover. Maybe I shared too strongly my discomfort with my friend Marj, a known troublemaker.

When the wedding weekend began, Richard and Beth arrived. I looked fantastic. If not exactly drooling, I could tell Richard was smitten. I made excuses to get Richard alone on the pretense of discussing the upcoming wedding details. Oh, we talked about table arrangements and the like, but it was all a cover. I took every page out of every vamp movie I had ever seen and played it to the hilt. Richard caved. He followed me around like a puppy waiting for its reward. I was satisfied. I didn't want him back. I just wanted Beth to know I was there first and wasn't going anywhere.

My friend Marj bestowed the final blessing. On the day of the wedding, she and Beth showed up in the same dress. It was a green paisley silk print specially designed for the mature woman. I would love to be able to tell you I was sorry for Beth and immediately rushed to console her, but I can't because I wasn't. It was a fateful accident that I thought was a sign that the gods were sympathetic to my feelings. Beth and Lee wandered aimlessly throughout the wedding weekend like two lost souls. I didn't even know Lee was there. Shame on me!

Lee and I pretended we were not approaching the end of our relationship. We knew better.

Lori and Rob were married not quite a year later in Puget Sound. Puget Sound is one of the Godspots of the universe. Views of the water against the backdrop of the Cascade Mountains. It seemed wherever I was... on a boat, on a promenade, from any one of the many islands surrounding the Sound, it was picture perfect. Richard and Beth's marriage was old and accepted news. No acting out was necessary.

It was a Quaker wedding. We non-Quakers sat in utter bewilderment while the congregation, in silence, waited to be "moved" by the spirit to speak. In my ignorance, I thought someone forgot their lines. On the radio, dead air is death. I was about to stand up and sing *You're Nobody Till Somebody Loves You*. Dianne and Pamela and their frantic eye signals saved me from embarrassing humiliation.

Pamela and Joel had always seen themselves as lawyer and advocate for the dispossessed and disenfranchised in a town of a size where their work would make a difference. They found it in Northampton, MA.

Lori and Rob had been living in Seattle, but Lori wanted to be closer to family on the East Coast. She convinced Rob to move to Northampton. It was great for me. One visit for the sight of two daughters.

Dianne was doing her tango with various men from all over the world.

The weddings took up much of the two years since I had returned from L.A... I was restless. I missed the natural geography that I had when I lived in California. There's plenty of nature on the East Coast, right?

My dear relative, who gave me her apartment when I was in *Ballroom*, had a little house in Bridgehampton. I was allowed to stay periodically and easily understood why the Hamptons and Montauk were a haven for artists. The light, extraordinary as it was, had almost as many moods as I did. The changing tides and sounds of crashing waves were new music to my ears. Was this Brooklyn girl capable of leaving the city? Of walking into nature instead of an elevator, giving up the subway for a walk on the beach? For the first time in my almost 60-year-old life, I could afford to give it a try. I had money in the bank to buy a house. Maybe if I moved to a quiet place I might be able to concentrate on writing and not the ongoing painful dissolution of my partnership with Lee.

I found a rundown house in East Hampton. It was a beautiful bayfront property. Could I afford it? It had major leaks in every conceivable nook and cranny. Nothing worked. It had little animals living everywhere. It was a wreck. With a lot of wrangling and with various scenarios from accountants and financial advising, I could swing it. A miracle. My dear friend, Ron, who left the theatre to become a builder, agreed to do the renovations.

Before we began, Ron asked,

"What do you want?"

I looked around to see who he was asking.

He was asking me. Other than a waiter at a restaurant, no one had ever asked me what I wanted.

I was bewildered. I didn't know what to say. I'm not sure I knew what I wanted. For the next few weeks, Ron and I worked on a wish list and a design. Some things were possible, others not. I didn't care.

Rebuilding that house was one of the most glorious creative experiences of my life.

~~~~

My British friends, Mary and Barry, had also caught building fever. They were in the process of converting a chicken house in Southwest France, between Toulouse and Bordeaux, into a vacation home. They had invited Lee and me for Christmas festivities.

It seemed to me the perfect solution. Rather than be with family who were aware of the direction our relationship was going, we would be with many people who knew and didn't know each other and who didn't know us. We could spend most of our time together, separately. We wouldn't be pressured to present a facade of the happy couple.

As the actress, I was better at hiding my discomfort than Lee. We knew the clock was ticking. We flew to Paris for New Year's Eve.

After sex, in my experience with any heterosexual male, my major job was to keep conversations and life lively and interesting. No dead air. Pretending had been hard work. I was exhausted. So was Lee.

We sat in a restaurant across from each other. We didn't speak a word. Not one. I don't even remember asking for the salt. Nada!

A day later, we flew back from Paris to NYC. En route, in the car, first to Lee's apartment, then onto mine, I said to Lee, "It's over."
Without so much as a pause, he replied, "Yes."

What was there to say? Over 12 years, we had said it all. Like my divorce, ours was a nobody's fault breakup.

Without the help I received from friends and Al-Anon, I would never have been able to see and understand my contribution to our denouement. There is no moving forward, no possibility of change without that knowledge. I had to know and acknowledge the role I played, or I would just continue the same punishing behavior as before.

One day, after a monster shouting match, the cuckoo in the clock with a hammer in his hand flew out of his nest and hit me on the head... hard. I finally understood: It wasn't me as an adult who was engaged with Lee. It was my abandoned three-year-old, too terrified to close my eyes, afraid of disappearing, who was screaming at him. I don't care if it is Psychobabble 101. It removed the bars from a window into my life, and I could see myself clearly.

Talk about a hallelujah moment!

I tried to make him understand. He would hear none of it. Instead, when I refused to yell and scream at him as I usually did, he accused me of not loving him anymore. I couldn't believe it.

"What's the matter with you? You like being yelled at... abused?"

LIGHTBULB!

Yes! He did like it. So did I. It was the language, the "love" talk of our childhood homes.

Punishment and guilt equals love.

I was no miracle worker. I could not change the past. I knew love couldn't be bought. Tried that. Therapy made me aware, yes. But that's intellectual. Love is so much more. It's organic, cellular. It's love. Damn it!

We arrived at Lee's apartment first. He stepped out of the car and out of my life.

I busied myself preparing to move to East Hampton, running to auditions, writing, and organizing performance dates for yet another version of Harriet.

Barely two weeks had passed when Lee's son David called.

"Sally-Jane, I'm in the Emergency Room of NYU Hospital. My father had some kind of attack. And I don't know what to do."
"What kind of an attack?"

"I don't know. I don't know."

"David, calm down. Call your sisters."

"No one is home."

"David, you must know your father and I aren't together anymore."

"I know. I don't know what to do. I don't know what to do."

I taxied over to the hospital. Lee was still on a gurney in the corridor. He was *not* happy to see me.

"What are you doing here?"

"David called."

"He shouldn't have."

"I know, but he did. What's wrong?"

"Don't ask what's wrong if you don't want to get involved."

From that moment, against everything I thought I knew, through to the beginning of the next year, I *was* involved. His adult children backed away. They had gone through trauma with their mother's illness and death. They may not have wanted me at Thanksgiving dinner (Isn't it terrible how long we hold onto stupid things?), but it was OK to let the take-charge-lady-of-everyone's-life take charge of their father's illness.

After the first months of tests, tests, and more tests, some serious diagnoses were happening. A brain tumor required surgery.

Malignant.

Terminal.

Hospital stays for treatment and further diagnosis.

When I wasn't moving to East Hampton, I was at the hospital. I wasn't a relative. I wasn't a spouse. I wasn't even a significant other. I was someone who loved and cared for him. In hospital terms, that wasn't enough to matter or to allow me to be confided in.

One day, I came into the hospital. Lee was very ill. They had begun a new series of treatments. It is known, and it is written... If cancer doesn't kill you, the treatments will. I was angry. I called the doctor who authorized the treatments and told him whatever he was doing was hurting Lee, not helping him. He agreed to look at the protocol. I walked back into the room. Lee screamed at me.

"You are killing me."
"What are you talking about?"
"How dare you call and question the doctor!"
"I did that because I've never seen you so sick."
"It's none of your business. These doctors know what's best. If you keep interfering, they won't cure me. And it will be your fault."

I walked out of the room, out of the hospital, down the street, talking and yelling to myself like city crazies do. With steam pouring out of my earballs, I went into a phone booth and called a dear friend.

"Maggie! I can't believe what just happened. I tried to save the idiot. I really did. He was sick as a dog from what they were giving him. I mean *really* sick..."
"Sally-Jane! Why are you there?"
"What do you mean why am I there? I am there to help him."
"Well, then, I think you better leave."
"What are you talking about?"
"If you are there for him. He's got you. No matter what you say or do, he can get to you."
"What does that even mean?"
"If you are there for *you*, if you walk into that hospital... into that room for *your* needs, *your* wants, no matter what you do, he can't hurt or harm you. On the principle of when you're flying, you are told to put the oxygen mask on yourself *first*. How can you help anyone if you're not breathing?"

Don't you hate it when someone sticks a pin in your ego balloon?

Slowly, I walked back to the hospital and into Lee's room. He was surprised to see me.

"I thought you left for good."
"It's not going to be that easy to get rid of me, honey."

"I know you. If not now, you'll leave soon."

"My dear. If you can say that, you don't know me at all."

And, in fact, he didn't, and neither did I. But I was beginning to know me. I never got the ratio right: sharing love and caring for Lee without surrendering to his moods and terror.

We were not a couple. Periodically, he wanted more. "Let's move in together." I reminded him, "It didn't work then. It won't work now."

It was February 1993. They began Lee's morphine drip. I remember asking the nurse if he could hear me. I'll never know whether I asked for me or for him. She nodded yes. I sat on his bed, lifted him onto my lap (he weighed nothing), and sang the whole *Rodgers and Hart Songbook* to him. All our favorite songs. I'd like to be able to tell myself he heard and smiled the whole way through. When I want to make myself feel better, I do. Honestly, I don't know. If he heard, great. If not, that was ok, too.

I was doing the Maggie thing. I sang the songs for me.

He died in my arms. His family's reaction to his death was completely appropriate. I never saw any of them ever again.

His obituary listed his 15 years before deceased wife, his children, not sure if his sister was mentioned, possibly his lawyer and accountant... kidding. What can I tell you? It was Thanksgiving all over again.

If I wasn't mentioned in the obit, I wasn't invited to the funeral, right? Friends of Lee's and mine gathered in my new/old house to celebrate his life. As easily as his chapter opened in my life thirteen years before, it closed with profound sadness and gratitude.

I lost a dear friend. I was present when he left.

For those not Brooklyn-born or Coney Island smart, the Cyclone is not a climate change happening but an amusement park ride. It was unauthorized therapy during childhood. As the Cyclone climbed and dipped, I loved screaming until my vocal cords gave out. This gave me a peace I never found at home. Today, scream therapy in a closet is more convenient than taking the subway to Coney Island.

There have been many cataclysmic events that gave me pause and changed my life. They paled into insignificance against Lee's death. I swear, holding him in my arms as he took his last breath turned my world upside down. Life is a great leveler. Death is greater.

Thanksgiving? What's the fuss? Just another day.
Stardom? It'd be nice. But is it necessary... you know, like food, clothing, or shelter?
Love? Aye, there's the rub. Without it, nothing works.

41

The Last Wedding and The Last Man

B y the time Dianne had a serious candidate in mind for the altar, Richard and I had a gaggle of grandchildren. Lori and Rob had three – Shira, Eli, Bayla. Pamela and Joel had three – Isaiah, Gabriel, Talia.

There is no better healer for grief than new life. Holding a newborn in my arms was the ultimate thrill and blessing. I loved my new job as Nana. Give them anything they asked for (almost) for the hug, the kiss, the squeeze, until old enough to escape my clutches.

Dianne surprised us all. After dating exotics from all over the world, she met Jim, a solid midwesterner. The perfect yin for her yang. The last of my daughters walked down the aisle in 1997.

Another beautiful wedding, this one on a farm in a 19th-century restored barn. By the time of Dianne and Jim's wedding, Beth and I were new best friends. No acting out on my part. She and I had adjusted to Richard's Solomon.

When I think of the next 30 years, I am reminded of my first colonoscopy. Awake but nicely loopy, I watched the screen as the doctor illustrated why my colon caused me so much grief. He pointed to the anatomy of this organ. First, it went to the right, then to the left, and then it hit a cul-de-sac, curling onto a roundabout. I had a curly colon. And so went the next thirty years. A few rights, a few lefts, some cul-de-sacs, some roundabouts... if an opportunity came up to travel, I took it. If an opportunity came up to do my show I took it. If an opportunity came up for me to be the Nana, I took it. If an opportunity came up to read, write, experience, and/or experiment, I took that as well.

I hadn't detached from my need for a male rescuer completely, but I was getting closer. Dating apps were a boon for me. Most of my life, I was an award-winning people pleaser. I lost count of all the times I said yes when I wanted to say no. It was thrilling when a "match" responded to my profile, and after reading his profile or even meeting for tea or coffee with new and growing confidence, I said no more than I said yes. Of course, this worked both ways, but as the nail said to the hammer, "What I don't know won't hurt me."

I decided to write my own satirical take on my dating app experiences using, of course, my alter ego, Harriet Ferment. I imagined Edith, Harriet's oversexed friend, introducing her to her latest "hottie," the dental hygienist Victor Veritas. They exchanged profiles. They met for tea a few times.

Scene: Harriet on the phone with Edith after her "date" with Victor Veritas.

"Thank you, Edith. Victor was a very important experience. It's so interesting because when I was a child, I had a lot of cavities. Too many Hershey Bars and Baby Ruths. My mother was always anxious about my dental bills. She suggested I save money by marrying a dental hygienist. Isn't that funny?

"Victor seemed very nice and ultra-polite. The perfect gentleman. He wanted me to come to his apartment. My teeth needed cleaning, so I suggested we go to his office first. It was a tricky way to get to know him, right? And just like you said, Edith he did a fabulous job. He wouldn't stop badgering me until I agreed to come to his apartment. I was a little nervous, but I remember you went to Victor's apartment...

"You're still here... right?

"I rang the doorbell. He answered, dressed in a very tasteful wetsuit.

"No, I don't think he was wearing fins. Not everyone looks good in a wetsuit, right? He looked great.

"Don't push me, Edith. You want to hear all the details, don't you? Well, next, I took off my coat and put it on what I thought was a mushroom stool. It wasn't. It was a sculpture. Victor called it 'Hiroshima'. How was I to know, Edith? It looked just like the mushroom stool Ikea sells for the bathroom.

"I have to tell you, Edith, it's a very unusual apartment.

"Well, it just was. He didn't have one stick of furniture in it... not one... except for a huge fur-covered mound. And you're gonna die, Edith. When I touched it... it moved. It did so. It moved. It was a waterbed. He must have bought it after your last visit.

"Wait, I'm not finished yet. Near the bed was a revolving red spotlight. I couldn't believe it. I asked him right out if he was going to give me a speeding ticket. Wasn't that funny? I made up that joke right there on the spot. I couldn't believe it, but his wetsuit was the same color as the spotlight. Bright red like an ambulance. When I turned around, he pushed a button, and a trapeze dropped from the ceiling and swung over the water... I mean the water bed. That was it for me.

"Well, Edith, we're just different. You've had a lot more experience than me. Leave it at that. And I did not spoil it for your date next week. I was very polite and complimentary as I backed toward the door. I told him that his teeth-cleaning techniques weren't the only thing that was unusual about him. It's true, Edith. No one had ever massaged my neck and my shoulders to relax my gums.

"I agree with you completely, Edith. I can't think of a better way to fight tooth decay. I never even knew I was getting flossed."

The desperate need to prove myself was becoming less and less of a driving force in my life. Of course, age had something to do with that, but if I were really honest with myself, which I could now afford to be, financial independence was challenging and, at the same time, changing my life. After Lee's death, my new friend Lynn had also recently lost her partner. An airline was selling around the world tickets. Each of us bought a ticket. I was heterosexual. She was homosexual. I had only traveled with heterosexual men, Richard and Lee. Lynn and I circled the globe, and I discovered I preferred a woman as a travel mate. I wanted to rewrite the song from *My Fair Lady*: *Why can't a man be more like a woman?* She wasn't offended when I didn't accompany her on an ultralight glider. I wasn't offended when she didn't want to meet some guy I had picked up on a glacier in New Zealand. If she didn't want to do what I wanted to do or vice versa, nobody pouted. We shared feelings.

Here's a generalization to chew on. Men don't like being asked how they feel. Why? They don't want to talk about how they feel because they don't know how they feel. If they don't know how they feel, it's because they don't talk about how they feel, so please do not ask them how they feel. Phew! In *The King and I*, Yul Brynner voiced it perfectly; *it's a puzzlement.*

Living in East Hampton and still auditioning in NYC or performing cabaret or one-woman shows was becoming more difficult. I didn't have a chauffeur or own a helicopter. Most pathetically, I made a mistake buying the house on a variable rate mortgage, so in the late '90s, when the stock market dropped, I literally could not afford to pay my mortgage. When it came to money, I still needed watching.

Marj, my friend who spoke her truth whether you wanted to hear it or not, lived in a wonderful apartment building in midtown. Because of the financial slump, apartments in NYC were actually affordable. I sold East Hampton and, after paying off the mortgage, with the little that was left, bought my first and only apartment in NYC across the street from MOMA and around the corner from Carnegie Deli. What could be bad about the new Carnegie Deli combo, pastrami over Picasso?

After their wedding, Dianne and Jim set up a home in an apartment in NYC and immediately went to work, increasing the world population: Kiri and then Ellie.

I was living in one of the greatest cities in the world, partaking and participating in the many gifts it had to offer. Traveling to the far corners of the world. Surrounded by a loving family. Without the complications of a relationship, life was pretty damn good.

However, I'm part of the human condition. Like the television show *Mission Impossible*, my mission, should I choose to accept it... is to complicate my life.

42

To Be a Star or Not To Be a Star???

(That became the question)

Some cultures don't fear death; they celebrate it. I feared death. What a waste of time. As sure as I was born, I was going to die. It was how I chose to live that would make the difference. Nice words. But did I really believe that, or was it just something I told myself when I awoke in the middle of the night all alone, waiting for the Grim Reaper to make a selection?

I was alone.Drum roll...That was getting to be O.K.I couldn't believe it.

Was I going through a more intricate and involved form of denial? With the way my mind worked, anything was possible.

New thoughts borne of new realizations. Cecil B. DeMille had obviously lost my address. It would have been more difficult for him to find me anyway. I lived on the eighth floor of a midtown apartment. Without getting past the doorman, it would be very difficult to see into an eighth-floor window to watch me dance.

Why was I limiting myself to NYC for the few auditions I was being called for? I was nearing seventy. Opportunities for parts for women my age were not only limited but I was auditioning against also-unemployed but well-known actors. If you had a chance to hire Angela Lansbury, would you even glance at my resume?

No big deal.

I'm lying. It was a big deal. It wasn't only the business that was giving me the business about my age. My palpable fear of death was also giving me the business. To put it bluntly, Mel Brooks's *Two Thousand-Year-Old Man*'s Angel From Death was stalking me. I bought extra garlic and kept my windows closed. It's not as if I was unfamiliar with death. The version of death I had from the time I was three never really left me alone.

In my sixties and seventies, I could still get on a dance floor and embarrass family and friends with my calisthenics. The energy was there. The opportunities for performing other than on a party dance floor... disappearing.

While waiting for my agent to call, I had the time to do some serious reworking and rewriting of Harriet Ferment. My relationship to Harriet was changing. I accepted that she was more than a shadow of me. She became an ongoing reflection of my personal "awakenings."... i.e... Victor Veritas. She was still outrageous. As her world collapsed around her, she continued to insist her life was perfect, perfect, perfect.

I wrote the following telephone monologue between Harriet and her mother based on a sense of the emotional and psychological confusion of mother/daughter relationships.

"Hello?

Oh, Hi, Mother. As usual, your timing is perfect. Perfect. Perfect. Perfect. I was just cramming for my bar. Having a little mother/daughter with Nina.

Am I my baby sister Carmen's keeper? She and my hubby Franklyn are at a succulent convention in Las Vegas.

Yes! I know. Franklyn saved her life by giving her that job. Her size five figure and flawless complexion didn't fool me for a minute. Five marriages. None of them lasted more than five months. She gives new meaning to that horrible disease of codependency. But I do what I can to help.

Please, Mother, I am not a pioneer. A middle-aged weight watcher in search of a career, yes! A pioneer, no! Besides, Daddy always wanted a lawyer in the family.

Yes, it's a real shame.

Hey! No more living in the past, remember? You're 68. You look 48. You're in better shape than I am. If it's any comfort to you, Daddy's death was the final push I needed to finish Law School. They never should have given him that driver's license. And when I become a lawyer mother, I'm going to sue to change the eye chart. You know, Mother, I only hope what I'm doing inspires you to do something with whatever is left of your life.

I've got to get back to the books. Did you call to tell me something?

Uh-huh! Uh-huh! Uh-huh!

You're having a facelift? You're kidding. What for? You don't need it. You don't.

Come on! How many times were you mistaken for Golda Meier? Just a joke.

Don't be silly. If that's what it takes to make you relevant, you do it. I hope you checked with your doctor. Unnecessary surgery, a woman your age, you can't be too careful.

Mother! Really! Why didn't you tell me you had a reason?

Uh-huh! Uh-huh! Uh-huh!

You're having an affair?

Catered?"

Harriet needed protection. I was her creator. It was my job. I became her bodyguard. And I began to fall in love with her. It changed the tenor of the show. Of course, I wanted the audience to like Harriet (me), but if they didn't, it was all right. Why? Because *I* liked Harriet (me).

I missed sunrises and sunsets. The call of the wild was becoming as necessary to me as ordering carry-out from Carnegie Deli. I found a small rental in the yet undiscovered town of Great Barrington, Massachusetts, in the Berkshires. An hour from Lori and Pamela and their families. It was the perfect distance for keeping my distance. In NYC, I had the perfect combo: my pastrami sandwich fix and visits to Dianne, Jim, and family.

43

Game Changer

M y neighbors and I called the eighth floor of our apartment building *The Dormitory*.

Over the fifteen years I lived there, three out of the five apartments on that floor were occupied by close friends. It was a weird combo of private and communal living. When the occasion arose, and one of us or the other was out of town, and an extra room was needed for visiting guests, we shared apartments, one with the other. We had dinners together. We went to the theatre, opera, ballet. We traveled together. We knew each other's families intimately.

It was the morning of September 11th, 2001, and it was my neighbor Bruce's birthday. My other neighbors, Bill and Cornie, and I bought a cupcake with a candle singing *Happy Birthday* as we walked to Bruce's door. Grim-faced, he opened the door and told us to go home and turn on the television.

Unbelieving and unable to talk, I stared at the transmitted images for hours.

I needed to see Dianne, Kiri, and Jim. I had to see them. I had to touch them. I had to know they were alive.

All forms of transportation in NYC were suspended. The once-busy streets of the city were eerily empty. No horns, no sirens, no airplanes overhead, no people. Slowly and silently, in a city that never sleeps, I walked uptown several miles to where Dianne and her family lived.

Once I arrived, I couldn't stop holding onto them. On automatic pilot, we placed Kiri in her stroller and walked out to Broadway. It was raining ashes. Without subway services, survivors made their way by foot to their homes. We watched a parade of zombies covered in ashes, dazed and in silence, walking by.

Dianne and her family were safe. Lori and Pamela were in Massachusetts. I know it didn't make any sense; they were out of the danger zone. I didn't care. I needed to see them for myself.

Transportation to and from the city was being shut down. The last train was leaving Pennsylvania Station for Hudson, NY, the transfer station for points north to Massachusetts. It was sold out. I walked down to the track. I begged and pleaded with the conductor. He said I'd have to stand. I said I wouldn't have it any other way.

A great deal has been said and written about 9/11. No one ever asked for my opinion. However, it would go against my religion not to open my big mouth.

Until then, the United States had escaped attacks on its continental footprint by foreign, cowardly, and evil terrorists. This is not a political statement; it is a statement of fact. On 9/11, radicalized crazy people caused the death and destruction, not of the military and military installations but of workaday people, flight passengers, and countless heroes and heroines of every service, most having no serious political agenda.

Several days later, as the world poured its empathy, sympathy, compassion, and condolences into the United States, I had a single thought: *This is it. Everyone talks about world peace. In light of these unspeakable horrors, these heinous attacks could be the perfect opportunity to make a peace that would surpass all understanding.*

What was I thinking? Didn't they promise the same peace after Hiroshima?

I really miss being able to blame a lot of blameable politicians. I am getting older. Blame is useless; it is wasted energy and time. I looked at my watch. I didn't have the time. I had miles to go before I slept.

Take a deep breath. Release it. Keep hoping.Chalk it up to another miss for the Human Condition.

44

The Only Constant Is Change

O h boy, what a cliché! Alright, already by this time you know my story is on cliché overload. But let me explain to you what I and the author, Patrick DeWitt, think about clichés. A character in his novel *French Exit* exclaimed: *Yes, my life is riddled by cliché, but do you know what a* cliché *is? It's a story so fine and thrilling that it's grown old in its hopeful retelling.*

Show me a cliché. I'll show you a truth.

It took a lot to unseat me from my pledge of allegiance to live in New York, New York. Splitting my time between NYC and the Berkshires, I had discovered a thriving theatrical community north of the great white way. I found various venues to exhibit my wares.

The Guthrie Center, which was the former Trinity church where *Alice's Restaurant* was filmed, became one of my favorite spots. Sometimes, I'd perform yet another version of Harriet Ferment. Sometimes, Harriet shared the stage with local talent in a modern vaudeville. I also found another house to renovate. My dance card was full.

I now had eight grandchildren. This latest remodeling job was designed to be their house and playground. Nearly every weekend, they came to play games, to swim, to toast s'mores, to climb up into the fantasy tree house a gifted fantasist built.

Shira, the oldest grandchild, was a baby just a few years ago, and by the time the treehouse was built, she was already in middle school. One of my favorite literary and theatrical characters was Auntie Mame. As I introduced each of my grandchildren into my world of theatre, music, dance, I became the Brooklyn version of Auntie Mame, aka Nana. At very early ages, they had attended many of my performances. Their pump was primed. I watched as the magic of the performing arts wove its spell over their growing bodies, hearts, and minds. With some of them, the soccer ball or gymnastics bar won out over any theatrical outing. With others, it was a hand-in-glove fit, and to this day, going to the theatre or, the ballet or a concert is a glorious tradition. I was also amused as I watched these beautiful earthling grandchildren navigate, aka manipulate, their various pursuits, their parents, and their Nana. They provided my world with a fascinating display of the varieties of human behavior.

As a septuagenarian, winters were becoming more and more difficult for me. I had tried Florida for a week or two. My sister Arlene lived in Longboat Key. Nice. After 9/11, my friend Marj moved to Naples. Nice. Neither location floated my boat.

I discovered my Shangri-La on Sanibel Island. A thin strip of land, only ten miles long and just a half mile wide. It had little commercial development but an abundance of natural wonders: mangroves, swamps, shell beaches, uninterrupted horizons north to south, east to west. In short, paradise. It didn't take long for me to convert. Over the years, a few weeks turned to a few months, and finally, I found an old Florida house to turn inside out. I sure loved to mess around with old houses.

What better way to introduce myself to the Island than by introducing them to Harriet Ferment? Over the five years I lived there, one or the other of us walked the beach, collected shells, and tried to fit in.

I did my last Sanibel show at their premier country club. They had everything except a stage. Not a problem. They cobbled together several platforms which when my friend and producer Lynnette saw what they built, announced it was an accident waiting to happen.

We didn't have to wait long. Twenty minutes into the show, I found the gap in the platforms and fell off the stage. From my place on the floor,

I exclaimed, "Can you believe I used to dance with Baryshnikov?" I was a senior member of the show-must-go-on union. The adrenaline shot up into my veins like a geyser, and I finished the show. One minute, I was taking a bow. The next minute, I was passed out on the floor. Somewhere in the vapor, I heard, "Call an ambulance." From where I was lying, It seemed like a good idea.

In any other location, an ambulance would have been the solution to the problem.

The Club was at the northern end of the island. You could sound the siren until you were blue in the face. It wouldn't matter. There were only two lanes. Going off island, either side of the road puts you into alligator-infested mangroves and swamps. Getting off the Island on a Saturday night was like getting into the right lane to go from East River Drive onto the Brooklyn Bridge... fuggetaboutit. Arriving at the hospital, the fog in my brainball disappeared. My leg was not broken, but I wore a badge of a colorful hematoma for several months.

My gerrymandered stage accident brought a new Sanibel awareness. I could have died trying to get off the Island. Added to that reality, friendships that I thought would last forever, frayed. At the best of times island living can be insular. Understatement. I'm an old Brooklyn gal who was comfortable living with a variety of human diversity.

I sold the house in Sanibel, but winter up north insisted on remaining cold and, icy and slippery. It became obvious that I wasn't finished with Florida. I am not a snowbird. I never saw a bird fly south with as much baggage as I carry. I moved from the west coast to the east coast.

Ain't it a bitch? I turned my head for a minute, and those little grandchildren became bigger grandchildren growing up and away from my playground house. Weekends were being canceled because of music lessons, karate, gymnastics, tutoring, team sports. Their changing world changed mine. If I could sell Sanibel, I could sell the playground. I did. Just when I thought it was safe to go back into the water, the universe threw me another fastball.

Dianne, Jim, Kiri, and Ellie, my NYC anchor, left for Baltimore. Overcrowded, overpopulated NYC was empty for me. I sold the NYC apartment. Except for the clothes in my closet, dishes and silverware in my cabinets, books, and CDs on my shelves, friends' and grandchildren's art on the walls, shoes on my feet, I didn't own a pot to... boil water in.

Cliché or not, this old lady was doing something I had only done in a classroom a very long time ago. Improvising. Amidst all this selling frenzy, I was making solo decisions. No man from Oz was behind a big screen commanding me to obey or else. No one from the male kingdom came forward to step on my feet. This reminds me - when I was in high school and college, I loved to go dancing. I was known for leading the male partner around the dance floor. If a man didn't want to be led, our blossoming romance was over. However, most of my partners had a not-so-hidden agenda...sex. If I gave them a signal of a possible score, I could lead them to hell and back without so much as a stumble. These last many years I had been without a partner on the dance floor or elsewhere. I was not unhappy. I was beginning to know me. Oh, boy, did I know me. I knew me well enough to realize it wouldn't take a micro-minute for me to return to my former codependent, controlling, freaky lady days.

Honey, don't worry, I'll make the reservations.
Honey, check your calendar. I put in all your dental, medical, and pedicure appointments for the next five years; God willing, you're still alive.
Honey, are you sure you want dessert?
Honey, you know I love Esther and Harold. I'm just reminding you that you didn't enjoy the last time we visited your children.

Keep it simple. Don't buy. Rent. Stay off the dance floor.

I found the perfect spot on a perfect small lake and like the dog lifting his leg to mark his territory, I have spent the next thirty or more years doing just that. I redid and continue to redo that lovely small house to my heart's content. My landlord and his family are part of my family.

They will be for as long as I and they are able. No matter where I go, this is home.

From my mouth to God's ears.
Gesundheit.
Hallelujah.
Thank you.
Amen.

45

Before I Forget... a few memories

*B*efore I Forget... *w*as the title of the last incarnation of Harriet Ferment, which I performed from my 80th year until my final show in my 84th year. Several years before, I watched as a very famous British actor, unable to remember his lines or where he should be, was moved like a chess piece about the stage by his fellow actors. I decided then I didn't want to be remembered for forgetting.

My British friends, Mary and Barry, had a vacation house outside the medieval wall town of Lectoure in southwest France. In the '80s, when they weren't "at home," they were kind enough to allow me to stay in their charming maison many times over the years. While there, I frequently ate at a favorite bistro in the tiny adjacent village of Terraube. In my broken French and their broken English, the chef and his wife and I became good friends. Good enough for me to give them a signed 8x10 glossy for their cafe wall. You don't honestly think at that stage of my life, wherever I went, so went a sackful of "just in case" headshots. I'd never forgive myself if, after all these years, Cecil B. DeMille suddenly showed up, and I was without my 8x10.

Flash forward. In the late '90s, Mary and Barry gifted Dianne and Jim with a stay at their home in France for part of their honeymoon. On my recommendation, they visited my friends in their Terraube bistro. They had a splendid dinner and, over a brandy, toasted my 8x10 that, unbelievably, was still on the wall. A British couple finishing their own brandy joined the conversation. Looking at the photo, the wife asked Dianne if the woman in the photo had ever done a show in Hampstead, England, several years ago. She described the show. Almost immediately, Dianne recognized Harriet Ferment. For a micro-moment, the roulette wheel of the universe stopped in a tiny bcite in downtown southwest France, and the past met the present.

I wrote Harriet Ferment thinking she would stay as young as me or as old as me forever. The wear and tear of my body parts snuck up on me. Bunionectomy? What the hell did I know about bunions, except that it proved we evolved from the apes? They were my first repairs. Next came knee replacements. Man, when it starts to go south, it's a fast ride.

I was being wheeled into the operating room for my first knee replacement. The anesthesiologist's selected music to work by was Dean Martin's *You're Nobody Till Somebody Loves You*. It was the song my father used to ask me to sing. It was a signature song in many of my shows. Under the influence, as they replaced my knee, in full voice, I accompanied Dean. Later, in the recovery room, the surgeon arrived to inform me of the success of the operation and asked me if I was available tc perform at their upcoming Doctor's Gala.

The body continues to send me messages that I consistently deny. Isn't that what denial is for?

I was living in one of this country's most beautiful natural environments, surrounded by some pretty fantastic cultural institutions. Tanglewood for classical music, Jacob's Pillow for dance, and several theatres for drama fans. My favorite place, though, is Edith Wharton's mansion, The Mount. I felt a kinship with this complicated woman who arrived late for her own awakening. She had a gift that was a challenge for one of her class and sex. At one time, The Mount was home to a theatrical group, so the idea of performing at the mansion was not a new one.

For the last many years, I have performed a variety of events at The Mount... one-woman shows, creative writing workshops, Wharton short-story readings, and holiday sing-a-longs. Along the way, I met the Executive Director, Susan Wissler, whose open-minded creative ideas and projects established The Mount as an important cultural destination in the Berkshires. Our affinities aligned, and she and her partner, Deborah, have become good friends.

Audiences varied from venue to venue and show to show, but no matter where or what I did, Richard was a steady customer. He didn't miss a show.

In the saga of Harriet Ferment, Harriet's husband, Franklin Ferment, was the stereotypical husband and father of the '50s, '60s, and '70s. If Harriet was my shadow, Franklin was Richard's. I wrote him as a satirically exaggerated character that was emotionally and psychologically stunted. His business was the sole focus of his life. He could never remember his daughter's name. He didn't have a problem with Harriet having an affair with his best friend. At Harriet and his 20th Anniversary party, he announced he was divorcing Harriet and eloping with Harriet's size five sister, Carmen. It was a caricature of the man I had married. If my life depended on it, I could not tell you why the man was *never* offended by what I wrote.

Richard sat through every show he ever attended like he was the proud poppa for everyone's enjoyment. The only sense it made to me is that somewhere in his jumbled but most brilliant brain, he thought of himself as Henry Higgins to my Liza Doolittle. Only I knew the years of abandonment while he was establishing his business were my most creative years.

My passion for the theatre ignited Richard's own love of the drama on and off the stage. In the style of Barnum, Ziegfeld, Steve Jobs, Richard Branson, et al, he was a businessman/showman. He wanted to be seen, to be known. My theatrical performances were opportunities for his performances.

I was doing a show at the Guthrie Center. Of course, he would be there. He had recently recovered from pneumonia.

"Richard, you've seen this show a million times. Beth agrees. Please take the time to really recover.""Before the show, Beth and I have reservations at a Berkshire spa. I'll be fine."

On arrival at the spa, he had some breathing problems and went straight to the hospital. I begged him to fly home as soon as he was able.

He'd think about it.

The evening of the show, as I was preparing for my entrance, Beth appeared wheeling Richard, oxygen tank in tow, into a clear area at the back of the house. I wanted to give whoever arranged his placement in the rear my personal blessings for not seating him in the front row.

Richard's spirit did not deteriorate with his health. He, too, had a big juicy bite for life. The many medical diagnoses Richard received didn't put a dent in his life energy or his humor.

As Richard's health declined, fewer and fewer pleasures were available to him. Driving was one he was never going to relinquish. There was no telling him that reflexes diminish with age. He refused to hear it. I challenged him,

"Hire a driver. What the hell is your money for if it can't help to save your life?"

My words zipped right past his mechanical earballs. So what else is new?

He didn't see the other driver as he was making his turn. The airbag exploded. Young and in good shape, people have survived the bruising and sometimes broken ribs of such an explosion. At 86, for someone of his precarious health, this was not possible.

Not long after the accident, his kidneys began to fail. He was forced into dialysis. The menage – Beth, Richard, and I, were out to dinner when Richard told a story of a friend of his who had to go on such a kidney machine. Eventually his friend decided it was not how he wanted to live. He quit the machine. He died.

You didn't have to be a rocket scientist to understand that Richard's story was for the wife and the ex-wife.

Beth was disturbed. I had heard it before. Not that particular story, but throughout our marriage and after, Richard never understood my palpable fear of death.

He would often warn me, "Sally-Jane, it's a fact of life."

"What has that got to do with anything?"

"I'm a pragmatist."

"You're Jewish."

"It means I am a realist."

"You're still Jewish."

"I love life. I know it is going to end."

"I *knew* it."

"I'm going to enjoy it as long as I have it."

"You don't love me anymore."

Here's the question that must be asked first... How did we last 27 years?

One thing you can say about Richard is that he was never subtle and he was telling this story to prepare Beth. When it comes to death, there is no preparation.

I don't remember if it was weeks or a couple of months from that dinner, but early one morning, a sobbing Beth called to tell me Richard had died.

There were no words. Holding onto the phone as if we were holding onto each other, we wept.

It didn't register for a while, but an era was over. I met this man when I was 18 years old. I was now 81. We lived so many eras of our life history together, apart but always within reach of each other. Lee's death left a sadness about what coulda, woulda, shoulda been. It was different with Richard. I created a special space within me that holds memories of our life together. If asked, I'll trot a story out for a laugh, a tear. If not asked and I'm lonely for him, I'll remember a moment when I was either more lonely or less lonely, depending on the state of our union. Weird as it sounds, we are still within reach of each other.

If I looked beyond the surface, without plotting or manipulating, this absurd trio was sustained, each in his or her own way because we came together in love. I am not talking about the kind of love we have for a person or things. There is a love that transcends the word love... a love that just.. is.

46

Love Is...

B ob Bendorf was a gifted composer and my music director for a few years. We had been through the wars together, personally and professionally. We met after my divorce from Richard. We had either met or knew each other's cast of characters. In my cabaret shows of the '80s, I wrote the sketches, and along with Shirley Grossman, he composed the music and wrote the lyrics.

His relationship problems were far more serious than mine. His lover left him after Bob was diagnosed with AIDS. Something terrible was happening to the homosexual population all over the world. I and the world around me was in the middle of a full-blown AIDS epidemic. Friends and acquaintances were being infected and dying. Most of the straight population existed in denial. It was a human and political disaster.

I spent the last two years of Bob's life learning how life and death can and do coexist. He never stopped working. I never stopped caring for him.

He had been searching for that book that would make him the next Hammerstein or Sondheim. He almost made it with a remarkable adaptation of *Great Expectations* for which he wrote the music and lyrics. There are so many genius projects floating in the ether for whatever reason that would never see the light of day.

We laughed and cried at the same things and because neither of us was very smart about relationships, time was spent discussing and diagnosing the whys and wherefores of love. In every language, in every culture, in every part of the human and animal consciousness someone has something to say or sing about love.

One night, sitting in my apartment, sipping wine and nibbling nibbles, after the pain had subsided from the first Thanksgiving debacle and after Bob's last lover left him, I asked,

"Bob, can you please tell me why when Lee or Richard or your Tom or anyone says, I love you, and they really believe they do, it's always just before they pull the rug out from under you. It boggles the mind because they really believe they do love you. What is that all about? And why the hell is that love not enough to keep the rug where it is? Why isn't love enough?"

Bob went home. He returned the next day. He had written a new song. Such a crazy idea. Love isn't person to person or a new car or shoes... like the universe, it just is.

Love is that simple
Love is that's all
How could it take me all these years to recall?
Those tiny moments that mean so much
An unexpected smile
A glancing touch

Love is so easy
Love is that's it
So many pieces and somehow, they just fit

So every time those little pressures start to grow
I will remember
It's all so easy
Love is
That's all I need to know

Love takes tomorrow
And makes it clear
Because the only time we know is right here
These precious seconds are just a taste
Of all that we could be
Or simply waste

Love is, that says it
Love takes the chance
Instead of sitting all alone
Join the dance
For it's a music much too lovely to ignore

I will remember
It's all so easy
Love is
Love is
Love is
There isn't anymore

Love Is, Music and Lyrics by Robert Bendorf

47

Is the Past Prologue?

W hoa! What happened? A minute ago, Richard and the other loves of my life were the bad guys. How did I change my tune? Give me a break, please. Allow me to do what the wooly mammoths in the L.A. Tar Pits didn't do... adapt... change. If you choose not to accept that change is possible, you ain't getting out of the tar pits either. I realize I can't tell anyone anything they don't want to hear. It's like our earballs freeze up. I have been forced to focus on my own "stuff." It's not as much fun as solving others' problems or telling people what to do, but it's easier on my blood pressure.

Recently I asked myself what was the point of holding onto the crappy parts of my life. What happened, happened. No matter what rabbit I pulled out of the hat, which I have never been able to do anyway, I was never going to be able to change what had already happened. Right?

Please, someone, tell me how holding onto the worst things that happened makes my life better. I figure a good half to maybe three-quarters of my life was based on memories of my three-year-old self's traumatic experiences. It put me and everyone in my life from the age of four to the present day in a self-created doghouse. Most particularly my crazy family.

How could I fault my mother for never having loved me the way I wanted to be loved when I know Dianne, Lori, and Pamela feel the same way about me? Is it even possible? To love someone the way they want to be loved.

In my family of origin, four boys, four girls, there were eight different versions of the mother and eight different versions of the father. No wonder no one listened to each other. Who could hear above the roar of the crowd?

On October 30, 1938, Orson Welles startled the world with his brilliant, mind-bending *War of the Worlds* radio broadcast. Our family was one of the many who believed it was a live news broadcast announcing that aliens were invading the Earth.

The reaction to the broadcast was orchestrated by an innocent and obviously extremely gullible mother and father. My oldest brother Raymond thought they were just plain dumb to believe such an unbelievable story. The good news is that they weren't the only ones. Across the country, thousands of families were doing the very same thing, escaping the aliens.

Each child had an age-appropriate reaction to the terrifying broadcast. Raymond, 18, curious and struggling to be independent, headed out on his motorcycle to pick up his girlfriend and check out the alien population. Our father threatened to take an ax to said motorcycle. In his brilliant Charlton Heston/Moses voice, he commanded his family:

"IF WE ARE GOING TO DIE WE ARE GOING TO DIE TOGETHER!!!"

Mad scientist brother Allyn sat in the car checking and rechecking his calculations. It was obvious to him the news broadcast was mistaken. His charts indicated the alien invasion wasn't until next year.

The broadcast announcer commanded the audience to drive to open-air parks. Orson Welles must have used some pretty interesting logic to convince his audience that open air was unhealthy for alien lungs. Prospect Park in Brooklyn was the closest safe haven for survival. This was the same Prospect Park that was known only for its proximity to Ebbets Field, home of the Brooklyn Dodgers. Lucille and Elliot were ordered to take pillows and blankets to the family 1937 Studebaker with extended jump seats. They took bribes and orders from their older siblings, filling the car with contraband comic books, makeup, favorite sweaters, Hostess cupcakes.

Marilyn was on the phone with her girlfriend Muriel, discussing alien availability. Each was sure meeting one of them would change their dull lives into the movie adventure they were craving. David took my hand, the one that wasn't holding my blankie while I sucked my thumb, and put me into my jump seat. Protectively, he sat next to me in his jump seat. Mother was in the kitchen, pouring her latest batch of chicken soup into clean, empty milk bottles. She also emptied the ice from the ice box. If the aliens made it into the house, she didn't want them tracking water all over her floors.

It's the little things that make for a comfortable evacuation. Mother called for Elliot to pack the chicken soup in the car and then picked up baby Arlene and headed in that direction. We were finally ready. Wait! Marilyn was still on the phone with Muriel. Dad almost blew a gasket. He commanded her name. The Red Sea parted, and out she came, practically in tears.

"They're not coming."
"Who?"
"The aliens."
"What do you mean?"
"The broadcast was a radio play by Orson Welles."
"What are you talking about?"
(Almost in tears) "I was on the phone with Muriel, and she heard the announcement that it wasn't a real news broadcast. It was fake. The whole thing was fake. The aliens aren't coming."

Slowly, one by one, the family disembarked from the car. Raymond was off like a flash on his motorcycle. Allyn muttered that he was right. Of course, there would be no alien invasion. It was too soon.

Lucille and Elliot pilfered the hostess cupcakes and comic books from their siblings. David took my hand, the one that wasn't holding my blankie while I sucked my thumb, and took me up to my bed. Mom took baby Arlene to her bed. And my father, who was probably the one who had listened to the broadcast and bought the whole damn alien invasion, was ever grateful that he wasn't the only one.

In 1938, on a Labor Day outing on the Atlantic City Boardwalk, an ordinary photographer took an extraordinary photograph of my family. No photoshopping. I saw what the camera saw. Anna and Louis's progeny, pictured in all their shining promise. The good life waiting for all of us just around the corner. If my mother was fearful of what was beyond her ken, I didn't see it in that photo. The years brought with them as many achievements as there were disappointments for everyone in the photograph.

As long as Mom and Dad were still alive, once a year, the Heit Olympics, aka family meeting, took place. The underbelly of this family occasion was the ongoing competition to win their love and attention. Remember in elementary school when we had a Show and Tell day? Heit family meetings were the adult version of that special school day. It was damn painful to watch as each of the siblings competed for the prize of best loved by reporting their awards, rewards, achievements, and gold stars. I remember at one of the meetings, one of my siblings had nothing to "report," so she brought her daughter's science project... an empty gerbil cage. Somewhere along the way, the gerbil had escaped. Lucky gerbil.

After their death, it was clear I was never going to be able to prove my mother and father loved me best. What the hell was the point of getting together? I wasn't the only one who thought the same thing. No more Heit family meetings. We would get together again whenever one of my siblings or one of the twenty-six grandchildren had a celebration... Bar or Bat Mitzvah, milestone birthdays or anniversaries, graduations, and weddings. Mom and Dad died within 18 months of each other. So did the family battery.

Raymond, Allyn, Marilyn, Elliot, Lucille, David, Sally-Jane, Arlene all shared a physical family resemblance; for me, that is where the similarity ends. We shared some interesting adventures, the *War of the Worlds* broadcast et al. But for me, after age three, I never felt part of the family. To me, my brothers and sisters were foreigners. Except for David because of our early trauma bonding. And for Marilyn because of our mutual passion for performing and her understanding, love, and help with my family and career. I didn't want to know who my brothers and sisters were. They didn't want to know who I was.

My thinking began to change while living in California. Brother Allyn was diagnosed with Parkinson's before the discovery of dopamine. Spending time with him before he died, I realized what I had missed by believing the family lies. Were we all doomed to be brainwashed, accepting the fearful pronouncements of our parental judgments? Not me. Previously a total stranger to me, I became very close to my oldest brother, Raymond, who recently passed away at 102 years of age.

I love them all very much, and I certainly miss them. I like to imagine how wonderful it would be to see all of them together at one more Heit family meeting. I'd like to think that whatever they said, whatever they thought, wouldn't make any difference to me. Of that, I will never be sure.

48

The Last Chapter?

W ho asked me to write a memoir?
Nobody!

Then why have I spent all this time writing about my life, my family, my friends, my not so friendly friends, my thoughts, my feelings, my everything?

Let's face it. I can't paint. I can't quilt. I can't tat. My knees won't let me garden. My toe shoes have been bronzed. What was I supposed to do with whatever time I had left on this planet? I do not want to admit it, but now that I ask me...

I am writing this memoir to keep Mel Brooks' Angel From Death from flying into my window.

I do not want to finish this memoir. If I finish this memoir, that damn Angel is going to find out where I live, and we all know what's going to happen next. So, pardon me if I use Penelope's suitor story as a metaphor for this memoir. You remember Penelope, wife of that philandering wanderer Ulysses.

Ulysses was off on his world cruise, all drinks included. Penelope was left at home to fend off suitors who were after her body and Ulysses' riches. She was no dummy. She needed to keep these suitors interested while she waited for Ulysses to tire of Circe, mermaids, and the like and come home and get rid of the suitors. What can I tell you? She was a one-man woman.

She decided to knit a scarf. She promised the waiting suitors that when she finished the scarf, she would choose her next husband from the assembled mob. Finishing the scarf was never going to be an issue. Every night, she unraveled whatever she had knitted the day before. No scarf. No choice. This Penelope was one smart cookie. And the suitors were pretty dumb not to figure out that every morning, she started knitting from the beginning. Really dumb. Ulysses should be ashamed he stayed away so long. Obviously, Penelope was a classic codependent. Otherwise, the *Odyssey* would definitely have had a different ending.

So there you have it. If Penelope could unravel the scarf every night, I don't ever have to finish this memoir. She was waiting for Ulysses. I have been waiting for death. No finished memoir. No death. Right?

Every few months or so I shall add another story, another character, another clove of garlic, to keep that Angel From Death from my window.

In the meantime, I am going to publish what I have written so far because I don't want my daughters to think I can't finish what I started. No matter how old they are, no matter how miscast I am, I'm still auditioning for Mother of the Year.

I've written a dozen different endings to this book. The problem is each one has a little nugget I want to share with you. As a Libra, I have always been very Talmudic... on the one hand... on the other hand.

Ending number one.

The journey with my daughters keeps making unexpected turns. As long as I am alive, it is a living, ongoing process. If there is one word that captures the process, it's... "surprise."

The ultimate betrayal for the girls, and for most children, was divorce. Mommy does not divorce Daddy without paying the piper. I have accepted a comme ci comme ça rating as a mother.

Being a Nana is different. I am a strange combination of fairy tale godmother mixed with a Lucille Ball zaniness, topped off with a dollop of Auntie Mame. When they were little we could be crazy together. As we grew older, I kept being crazy, and it was the grandchildren's turn to roll their eyes back into their heads, just like their mothers used to do.

I enjoyed being their Fairy Godmother, waving my money wand, sharing my share of Richard's money with them. It was the Auntie Mame of my nanahood that was my favorite part.

Auntie Mame and I concur; life *is a banquet, and most poor suckers are starving to death!*

My daughters are in their sixties now! What? Are you kidding?

You read about Dianne in my chapter about China. She kept to her world travels, making forever friendships wherever she went. Married to Jim, birthed Kiri and Ellie, surprising many a Chinese vendor anywhere she lands in the world when she bargains in Mandarin. She is needed to save faces, ours, theirs, the world.

Lori and Rob had Shira, Eli, aka Catsy (his contribution to gender-free identity), and Bayla. Lori and Rob divorced. Her story to tell if she so desires. She happily met and married Chris who added light to her life and brought joy and understanding to her and her children and her granddogs, Sophie and Tucker. She and Chris are beginning a new life, building a new home in a Co-Housing Eco Village. Lori has begun a two-year program to become an ordained interfaith minister. A perfect placement for her compassionate nature.

Pamela and Joel birthed Isaiah, Gabriel, and Talia. Though we were and are all born Jews and because Joel is a religious one, at the age of 58, Pamela decided to study and celebrate a Bat Mitzvah. A very different religious calling than the one she was raised in, where all holidays were celebrated. My church, temple, and mosque, which I shared with all my children, were housed within the Universe's natural wonders. Each of my daughters and their husbands continued their love of nature, but Joel and Pamela became leading members of their progressive and globally involved synagogue. Joel is a lawyer for low and moderate-income clients in cases involving tenant's rights and employee rights. Pamela is the Director of the Western Massachusetts Network to End Homelessness. In their separate endeavors Pamela and Joel are to this day politically and environmentally concerned humanitarians whose actions speak as loud as their words.

Dianne, Lori, and Pamela have strong opinions (inherited from both sides of the aisle). Like most of us they have been tossed around by life and have evolved as independent, compassionate, caring women with loving partners and children.

All right, already! I confess. I had very little to do with that. Way back... earlier in the memoir, I mentioned that the best thing I did for them was to get them into therapy early so they would see that their parents really didn't know what the hell they were doing. To my frustration, early in their lives, they established boundaries. This simple therapeutic tool allowed them to grow and develop into who they are and not into what I or Richard thought they should be. Hallelujah!

Ending number two.

Full disclosure. Yeah, alright, already. I had some issues with a few of my daughters' life choices. Stop pushing. Alright... more than a few. I am a very opinionated lady. And here is where my editor is screaming... *illustrate, paint a picture, show the reader*! Not on your life. You never found out how much money Richard left me. When it comes to the girls, whatever revelations I previously revealed, that's it!

Here is what I will share. *Love Is* is real and true. I experienced it. Dianne, Lori, and Pamela are my proof. Unconditional love is not love on demand or command. It just is.

Against the backdrop of life and death, as long as I know *love is*, I have the winning lottery ticket. Follow along with me if you dare.

Take your right hand... left hand... whatever preference... expose the inside of your wrist. Take the first three fingers of the opposite hand... place them on the inside of the wrist... and count with me... 1, 2, 3, 4, 5, 6, 7.... Did you feel a pulse? What's your problem?

Ending number 3

Like I said, I never thought of myself as a good role model as a mother, pretty good as a Nana, and not bad as a human.

Wake up, Sally-Jane! I am not just a mom. I am not just a nana. I am a someone else.

It's been a stratospheric tightrope walk from motherhood to nanahood to personhood. The possibility of falling off that tightrope is a constant reminder I hadn't yet made it over the precipices of life.

Did you hear the one about a guy who fell from a cliff and, before crashing to a certain death, grabbed onto a branch for dear life and shouted up to the top,

Help! Help!

This big booming voice shouted down to him,

I'll help you.
Oh, thank you.
The first thing you have to do is let go of the branch.

Long Pause...

Is there anyone else up there who can help me?

I enjoy escaping death. I would rather not be that close to the final event ever, ever, ever again...

And yet? Here I am as close as I'm ever going to get... well... *Not Yet.*

Acknowledgments

T his memoir has been a work in progress since birth. I hit 90 along the way, so I'd have to say a lot of people helped me complete the task. I could spend whatever is left of my life thanking all of those who helped me. And, by the way, I would have to include all those people who actively discouraged me. They served an important purpose. They motivated me... I'll show you... the repetitious chorus of my journey. Of course, I want to thank everyone who even remotely said or did an encouraging act of kindness and goodness. Still, I'm going to limit the number of thank yous because the book is finished, and at my age, I probably have a doctor's appointment.

That being said, I'm going to skip thanking those from the first eighty-seven years of my life and begin with those who helped me from the first time I put words to paper a couple of years ago.

Remember the skeleton song *Dem Bones, Dem Bones*, the foot bone connected to the leg bone, the leg bone connected to the knee bone, etc.? Well, that's how it was for me.

Martha Sherrill, beautiful person, and writer, connected me to Tamara Jones, beautiful person, and editor.

Good friends, first readers, and brilliant cheerleaders, Daniela Varon, Normi Noel, Deborah Dickman, Susan Wissler, Lynn Birks, Joni Carron, Barbara Leibovitz, Jaime Hellman, Vel Rankin, Ron Comenzo, Mary Fulton, Charles Westerfield, Cindy Sanford, Virginia Claus, Arlene and Ronnie Krum. And to my three beautiful cheerleaders, Dianne Lori and

Pamela, with a specific nod to Pamela for braving the unedited pages and not divorcing me.

Shout outs to Paul Ruben, Director, and Jason Brown, Engineer, for their artistry and generosity.

But the mostest, biggest thank you belongs to the head honcho, the chief, el presidente of the whole shoot'n match, Lynnette Najimy, introduced to me by Joni Carron, a dear friend whose fabulous laugh always makes me laugh. From the day Lynnette and I met 14 years ago, she has moved me like a chess piece from one project to the next. She believed in me as a writer when I only thought of me as a performer. She opened my world by establishing my *Blah, Blah Blog*, an enterprise that is perfect for the lady who always wants the last word. She brought me gently into the world of technology. Because of her, I can do anything except copy and paste. If you read the book, you know I'm not perfect.

As I performed my last one-woman show, Lynnette waited in the wings with a proposal for writing this memoir. She had to override all my fears about who would possibly be interested in any of my stories. She made all these brilliant moves and so much more with life-affirming kindness and humanity. We both have a profound agreement and understanding of life, as expressed by Niall Williams in his novel *This Is Happiness*,

...most of the moments of your life, stop one heartbeat, and no matter what the state of your head or heart, say this is happiness because of the simple truth that you were alive to say it.

There is no way I could have done any of this without any of you. That goes for the living and the dead of my humongous family: the good, the not-so-good, the beautiful, and the not-so-beautiful. Most especially to Marilyn Edith, my adored oldest sister, who blazed a trail for me in loving support; my recently passed 102-year-old oldest brother, Raymond. He was in the family from the time I was born, but I met him for real at his 80th birthday celebration; my last surviving sister, Arlene, and her husband, Ronnie Krum, who share with me aging war stories, old movies, and a love that's forever; and my beautiful brother and protector, David, aka "Al Jolson."

Thank you one and all for the greatest ride of my life. Oh, and by the way, there is no honorarium.

Visit Sally-Jane's website at
sallyjaneheit.com

Subscribe to *Sally-Jane's Blah Blah Blog* at
sallyjaneheit.substack.com